GRIPPED BY HOPE

DISCOVERING GOD'S LIGHT IN DARK PLACES

Tyrone P Jones

ENDORSEMENTS

"My good friend Tyrone Jones has hit a big home run with his latest book "Gripped by Hope." In a world that attacks our hope at the core, this book drives right through the middle of the noise and creates a pathway to rediscover hope once again. Hope is what sustains you, gives light to the future and builds the faith necessary to lift your heart and soul. Do yourself a favor and read this book and let hope rise again!"

Chris Sonksen
Author/Coach/Pastor, ChurchBoom, ChurchRescue

"What a joy it is to read and engage with this new book by Tyrone Jones, a great friend, a wonderful husband and father, a seasoned pastor and church leader, and a man who is deeply committed to Christ and the Gospel. In this book, he shares the back story of a life that has had a lot of twists and turns, highs and lows, blessings and challenges, but because of faith in the promises of God, and the hope inspired by that faith has grown from faith to faith. His personal journey will inspire you to hope again, not based on uncertainty, but on the rock-solid word of God. Enjoy!"

Bill Scheidler
Author, Executive Team Leader of Ministers Fellowship International, Founder of Church Leadership Resources

---

"We are engaged daily in "Spiritual Warfare". We are fighting for our faith, our souls, our children's souls, and hope of eternal salvation! Tyrone Jones has laid out a game plan for all of us to refer to in order to strengthen our hope, walk

ENDORSEMENTS

in God's presence, and bring Hope to others.Our Hope in God's plan for us must be strengthened daily. Not only does Tyrone do an excellent job of laying this out for us, but he walks the walk as well. I have lived this with him. He is a shining example of hope and God's grace."

Rhett Stallworth
President of Yuma Catholic High School

"Mental and emotional health are hot topics socially in the day in which we live. Tyrone Jones' book, " Gripped By Hope" gives us one of the Biblical keys to overcoming a major obstacle to overcome the maladies of our day-hopelessness. With 14.2 suicides per 100,000 people in the United States and 21 million Americans suffering from severe depression annually, " Gripped By Hope" gives a simple but profound answer to the maladies of our day. The antidote to being overwhelmed by life is hope, and as Tyrone has laid out for this in his life transforming book, Biblical Hope carries us, sustains us, and helps us see what is beyond us.

This Hope does not come from wishful thinking. According to Tyrone, the root of our issue of hopelessness comes from the fact that as humans, we have been absent from the presence of God. The answer to our dark moods and thoughts about life and ourselves has a spiritual root, therefore, a biblical answer. The key to this is recognizing the fact that God has opened to us a relationship and a life of wonderful promises because of what Christ did for us on the Cross.

Tyrone not only does a thorough job in giving us comprehensive Biblical answers to hopelessness but illustrations and stories of how he personally overcame the dark challenges of his life. As he has done in 35 years of pastoring, Tyrone leads us to the road to hope not just from the scriptures but from his own testimony of applying these truths.

This is not a light two hour read: it is a book that calls us to embrace the Word of God as the answer to the emotional challenges we face and to dig into its truths. This book calls us to do the work and to study. As Pastor Tyrone so eloquently says, " Christianity is a teaching faith, and our text is the Bible." Let's go to work and apply the truths this book lays out for in our journey to possess the full life of Christ. Thank you Tyrone for the gift this book gives us."

Bob MacGregor
Vice Chairman of Ministers Fellowship International (MFI), Founder of HIS Church

---

"There are many books that have broached the broad subject of hope, but you would be hard pressed to find one like Tyrone Jones, 'Gripped by Hope.' Within these pages, you will find pain, darkness, questioning, wrestling, yes- it's part of our human experience. But you will also unearth deep faith, unflinching expectancy & a resilience that can only come from the throne room of heaven. Tyrone writes with uncomfortable honesty, allowing the reader to truly enter in and find their own journey toward the 'hope against hope' the bible promises to us who love God & have been called to His purposes."

Raydeane Owens
Author: Heaven/Earth & Brave One , Co-Founding Pastor of The Heart, Coeur d' Alene, Idaho

---

"Tyrone moves, shares, guides, directs... All roads lead to hope being with Convoy Of Hope; we give help but want still hope through the local church into the community. Thank you for your faithfulness and continuing to lay out a pathway. I continue to gleam so much from you.

This book has been so directionally affirming Gods calling on my life and the mission of Convoy of Hope, to give help to instill hope.

Hope (knowing the destination of our path), tell others. Love this action "passively accepting what we cannot change and actively pressing on in faithful obedience and discipleship."

Hope, patient endurance, encouragement, hope, it will happen?! This book reminds us, we know it will happen!

ENDORSEMENTS

Awestruck expectation of empowerment to boldly live out Gods purpose. Hope brings joy "The shift from death to life not only fuels our hope, but it's also the seedbed of joy."

Thank you Pastor Tyrone for sharing your stories. May it bring hope through knowing Jesus Christ."

Rick Zorehkey
Partner Engagement, Convoy of Hope

"Years ago, I overheard a neighbor describe her 3-year-old daughter as a "serial optimist"—a child so full of joy and resilience that nothing could bring her down. I remember thinking, "What a reputation! I hope that's how people see me, too." For much of my life, I believed I carried that kind of presence. I saw myself as someone who brought hope into every room—a "hope dealer," just like the one Tyrone describes in this book. But that reputation was deeply challenged when our oldest daughter faced an 18-month, untreatable, life-threatening health crisis.

During that season, the psalm unpacked in this book—Psalm 42—became our anchor. David's words reminded us that God, and God alone, is our true source of hope. By God's mercy, our daughter has since experienced supernatural healing, but after reading this book, I can't help but think: I wish this resource had been available then.

In Gripped By Hope, Tyrone doesn't just point to God as our source—he invites us to rediscover why we can place our trust in Him. With heartfelt transparency, biblical depth, and redemptive storytelling, he offers what so many desperately need: a pathway back to hope that endures. This will be my go-to resource for anyone navigating a season that feels hopeless—because it restores what life so often attempts to steal: true hope."

Tim Bittle
Lead Pastor of TFH San Francisco

ENDORSEMENTS

"Gripped by Hope is exactly the kind of book our world needs right now. It's honest, wise, encouraging, and full of the kind of hope that is beyond wishful thinking. It's a hope that's rooted deep in faith, it's a hope that is tangible. My friend has written something that doesn't just inspire, it challenges. It gently calls out the fear and discouragement that so many of us quietly carry, and replaces them with the powerful, unshakable, promise of God that is hope. Every page points back to Jesus, and every page reminded me that even when life is difficult I could be "Gripped by Hope"."

Beau Norman
Lead Pastor of The Hill Church

"Pastor Tyrone P Jones has quickly become one of my favorite Kingdom voices. 'Gripped by Hope' couldn't be any more timely for our world today. Proverbs says, that 'hope deferred makes the heart sick.' We cannot live without hope—and Pastor Tyrone P Jones has packed every page with revelation and insight that is sure to help EVERY reader find light in life's darkest seasons."

Jordan David Ward
Singer/Songwriter, Consumed by Fire

"Pastor Tyrone Jones is a generational leader with a revelation on HOPE that is straight from Heaven. As a father of three kids that were given a terminal diagnosis, I have experienced firsthand what it feels like to be gripped by fear. However, after reading 'Gripped by Hope', I can see clearly how Pastor Jones charts a pathway for people to walk in true freedom despite their circumstances. I highly recommend reading this book that will cause you to live from a different perspective of not just hope but VICTORY!"

Matt Rogers
Evangelist, NFL Announcer (Tennessee Titans), LIV Golf Announcer

ENDORSEMENTS

"Tyrone's book, "Gripped by Hope," is an inspiring, practical, relatable, and intimate walk-through adversity. As Tyrone shares his firsthand experiences, we are given a roadmap that not only guides us through adversity, but, more importantly, shows us how to be genuinely transformed by hardship. As he so clearly states, "pain isn't wasted."

Tyrone's experiences with divorce, church conflicts, and life's loneliness have resonated with us. This book is an honest dialogue with a good friend, who out of love and respect for you and the truth, explains that disappointment, hurt, and disillusionment are unavoidable stops and detours in life's journey. There is no detour, no way around these obstacles, we can only go through them. The promise is that on the other side of the difficulty is transformation and an unshakable, immovable knowing that God loves me and sees me distinctly, uniquely, and is eternally devoted to loving me. The scriptures and practical application of their truth show the way through so that the pain truly "isn't wasted," but it is an investment in growth, healing, and liberty.

Thank you, Tyrone, for your honesty and for sharing God's truth that is like a spiritual GPS that will help us navigate through life's unfamiliar and challenging life experiences."

Jeff Howie
Training Director, YWAM Tyler

Vicky Howie
Bright Hope Coordinator, Love Mercy International

"'Gripped by Hope' is a powerful reminder that even in our darkest moments, God is at work—shaping beauty from brokenness. Tyrone's honest, hope-filled journey invites readers to discover the treasures hidden in their own trials and trust God's redemptive plan. His story is real, relatable, and full of the kind of hope we all need. If you're in a dark place, this book will remind you that God isn't done with your story."

ENDORSEMENTS

"He invites readers to find the treasures God forms in the darkest seasons. As a friend, I've seen the joy and strength he now lives with—proof that God truly restores."

Cara Grimm
Executive Pastor of Life Church, Walla Walla, WA

"Tyrone P Jones hasn't just written a book; he's written a lifeline. 'Gripped By Hope' is both deeply personal and profoundly biblical, guiding us through valleys that most pastors wouldn't admit to. As a fellow lead pastor and long-time friend, I've seen Tyrone lead with strength, humility, and unwavering faith. This book is raw and real about pain, but it's also filled with the hope that only Jesus can bring. If you're in a season where your faith feels fragile or your future seems unclear, this book will remind you that God is with you, and that truth is more than enough to carry you forward."

Dustin Woodward
Lead Pastor of Citizen Church, Chairman of Co-Church Network

"Life can hit us with a blindside sack, and spoiler alert: it's not energy drinks or sheer willpower that gets us through. It's HOPE. Real, soul-anchoring, God-given hope. In 'Gripped by Hope', we walk through Pastor Tyrone's life story of tackles, triumphs, and trust in a faithful God. His journey is raw, sometimes humorous, but always rooted in the kind of hope that only comes from the Lord. This book isn't just a testimony. It's an invitation to believe that with God, HOPE always has the final word. When God asks us to 'water dirt' you better believe a 'full lawn' is on the way! Pastor Tyrone opens up powerfully, showing that 'the hope of my calling is being lived out.' His message is obvious: when you find yourself fumbling, doubting, lost, lonely, or scared out of your mind, hear this loud and clear... 'you were not made for this.' GRIP HOPE."

Laura Dunn
YC Mom, CTC Member

"Gripped by Hope is an honest look at a Christian's life with its struggles and victories while focused on the hope Christ offers us. I found Pastor Tyrone's recounting of his journey with hope inspiring. If you're looking for encouragement in your walk with Christ, (and let's face it, we all are) this book will help you on your daily journey."

Douglas Nicholls
Mayor of the City of Yuma, Deacon at St. Francis Catholic Church

---

"Sometimes you meet someone and instantly know God placed them in your life for a purpose. For me and my family, that person is Pastor Tyrone Jones. This book feels like a powerful extension of the wisdom, strength and hope his preaching has poured into my life over the years. Gripped by Hope is more than a book, it's a divine spark. From the first page, Pastor Tyrone's words reflect resilience, the kind that's born in adversity and unwavering faith. His journey is real, it's vulnerable, and it's powerful.

Pastor Tyrone doesn't just talk about hope, he lives it. Through every setback and struggle, his trust in God shines through, reminding us that hope isn't wishful thinking, it's armor. This book speaks to the weary soul, the one who feels stuck, unseen, or unsure.

If you've ever questioned whether God still moves in impossible places, this book is your answer. Pastor Tyrone shows that when you surrender your story to God, He writes something greater than you imagined. Gripped by Hope is a call to rise up, believe again, and hold on tight, because the best chapters are still being written."

Robyn Pouquette
Yuma County Enterprise Risk Administrative Director, Flinn-Brown Fellow, Former Yuma County Recorder

Gripped By Hope
Discovering God's Light In Dark Places

Copyright © 2025 by Tyrone P. Jones
Published by:
In His Grip Media
Church For The City
Yuma, Arizona
United States of America

All rights reserved under International Copyright Law. No part of this publication may be reproduced or transmitted in any form or by any means, electronic or mechanical—including photocopying, recording, or by any information storage and retrieval system - without permission in writing from the publisher

Scripture Acknowledgments:
Unless otherwise indicated, all Scriptures are taken from the Christian Standard Bible®, Copyright © 2017 by Holman Bible Publishers. Used by permission. Christian Standard Bible® and CSB® are federally registered trademarks of Holman Bible Publishers.

Scripture quotations marked (NLT) are taken from the Holy Bible, New Living Translation, copyright ©1996, 2004, 2015 by Tyndale House Foundation. Used by permission of Tyndale House Publishers, Carol Stream, Illinois 60188. All rights reserved.

Scripture quotations marked (NKJV) are taken from the New King James Version®. Copyright © 1982 by Thomas Nelson. Used by permission. All rights reserved.

Hymn and Song References:
Lyrics from "Hope In Front of Me" by Danny Gokey used by permission.
Public domain hymns referenced include works by Charles Wesley, George Whitefield, Walter Chalmers Smith, Edward Mote, and others as indicated in the text.

Hardback ISBN: 979-8-9991693-0-3
Paperback ISBN: 979-8-9991693-1-0
Digital ISBN: 979-8-9991693-2-7
Printed in the United States of America

This book was published with assistance of Goodwill Media Services Corp,
www.goodwillmediaservices.com.

 Goodwill Media Services Corp.

Cover concept, design, and photography by Virginia Jones, Joel Jimenez, and Bili Escobar.

To Virginia, *my dear wife, best friend, and mother to eight children in a manner the Word of God portrays. Without her in my life—as the prayer partner and encouraging support—this book, nor the effective ministry, would be possible. Nor would the cover design and title exist, since they were her idea.*

To Church For The City, *which has grown to be—and proven to be—a church in our community that is salt and light! Each one of you who gathers there has given me hope in the goodness and promises of our God.*

To Andrew Torres, Frank Martinez, and Doug Bostwick, *the Senior Elders of Church For The City, who have fought the good fight with me and alongside me for three decades.*

To Bill Scheidler, *who has believed in me, instructed me, and encouraged me through over three decades of my pastoral ministry.*

And to my children *(Jermaine, Tyrone, Tecia, Tiffany, Malachi—and Norman) who lived through all that life brought our way—and even at its worst, gave me the reason to be gripped by hope!*

FOREWORD

Life without hope is not a life, it's just an existence. I am excited for you to read this book because I know the author well and have watched him navigate hopeless seasons in his life and ministry yet come out the other end of the "valley of the shadow of death" smiling and proclaiming, "the best is yet to come!" The following chapters will take you deep into the Word of God, as well as personal experience and testimony of what a life of unshakable hope can look like, and that life is for you. Biblical hope is not like common hope or low-level earthly hope where we 'hope we win the lottery' or 'I hope she says yes when I ask her out'. True hope is based on the credibility of the one who is making the promise of a better future. This kind of biblical, Christ-centered hope is unshakeable and becomes the anchor for our souls no matter the intensity of the storms of life or the temporary tragedies and seasons of uncertainty that touch us all.

Hebrews 6:18-20
New Living Translation

> *"18 So God has given both his promise and his oath. These two things are unchangeable because it is impossible for God to lie. Therefore, we who have fled to him for refuge can have great confidence as we hold to the*

hope that lies before us. [19] **This hope is a strong and trustworthy anchor for our souls.** *It leads us through the curtain into God's inner sanctuary.* [20] *Jesus has already gone in there for us."*

We all need an anchor! The image and reality of "the anchor for our souls" is something we must have in this life, or we will drift aimlessly down stream or out to sea. Without "the anchor" we will find ourselves at the mercy of every unexpected storm, unpredictable season of loss and pain or the confusion and disillusionment that comes through betrayal, divorce, abuse, financial collapse and all the other manifestations of evil that have temporary access to us on this broken planet.

Yet through it all we have the certain, unshakable promises of God's Word that are based on what Jesus has already accomplished for us. Yes, the work has been done, the cross of Christ is the ultimate victory, for all time and eternity, and His resurrection has become the foundation of our unshakable hope. The verse we read uses "temple imagery" to describe where our hope is anchored. When it says that Jesus has already gone to the "inner sanctuary for us" it is speaking of the unobstructed presence of God, the very place where God abides, our eternal destiny.... heaven.

This kind of access, and the confidence that comes with it, is not reserved solely for the second coming and eternity with Jesus. You can live in His presence right now and experience pure, unshakable hope. As you read the following pages you will have moments where the Holy Spirit will invite you into His presence. I would encourage you to take those invitation moments, sit the book down and spend a few minutes in prayer and worship with a journal nearby. As you do this, you will feel hope begin to arise, clarity for the future will come and you will sense the foundations of your faith and future being strengthened in real-time.

If you've been on the planet for a while you have realized that there are times when life just does not make sense. Especially if you are a believer and doing your best to live by the Word and trust Jesus with your future. When these seasons of confusion and pain come, and the unexpected storms are buffeting our lives, it causes us to examine our foundations and our hope.

Romans 8:28
New Living Translation

> *"And we know that God causes everything to work together for the good of those who love God and are called according to his purpose for them."*

Yes, it's a mystery and a miracle how God can and does use the worst that life can throw at us to accomplish His purposes in us. This does not mean the attacks we suffer are from the Lord. Many things in life fall into the category of "not good and not God" yet we hold onto a real and living hope that He is causing it all to "work together for the good"… Only GOD!

God uses the pain, delay, attack and even wicked people who mean us harm, to draw us into a deeper place, a more intense pursuit of Him and to run to the refuge of His presence where our hope is renewed. Yes, life does not always make sense, when we are looking through temporary lenses, but life always makes sense in His presence, and this is where we are Gripped by Hope!

Dave Patterson
Lead Pastor of The Father's House
Leader of TFH Network, ARC Lead Team

TABLE OF CONTENTS

Endorsements 3

Dedication 13

Foreword 15

Introduction 21

Chapter 1
Rediscovering Hope: Finding Light in Life's Darkest Seasons 31

Chapter 2
There's A Light: Finding God's Presence in Life's
Darkest Moments 43

Chapter 3
Eyes Enlightened: Discovering God's Purpose
Through Life's Seasons 55

Chapter 4
The God Who Is There: Finding His Presence in Our
Darkest Seasons 69

Chapter 5
Keep Walking: When Faith Requires Another Step 83

Chapter 6
There is an Enemy: Standing Firm When Darkness Pushes Back 93

Chapter 7
Faith Is Not A Fix: Finding God's Love in Seasons of Suffering 107

Chapter 8
Hope In Front of Me: Embracing God's Promise for Your Future 125

Acknowledgements 147

INTRODUCTION

*"I know in my soul no matter how bad it gets
I'll be alright"*

Several decades ago, the late German theologian Juergen Moltmann wrote a book entitled The Theology of Hope[1]. The whole idea behind the "theology of hope" is that believers have a hope which sustains and carries each believer through life. As stated in 1 Peter 1:3 (ESV), *"Praise be to the God and Father of our Lord Jesus Christ! In his great mercy he has given us new birth into a living hope through the resurrection of Jesus Christ from the dead."* It is an expectation that the promises of God are already in the process of fulfillment. Moltmann's point was that eschatology (the doctrine of the last things) should not be an appendix to Christian theology but should be the starting point of everything. According to him, it is confidence in what God is going to do in the future that must determine how we think and act now.

INTRODUCTION

I am not sure that is entirely right. While the theology of hope does have its value, its tendency to blur the lines between future fulfillment and current experience should be a cause of some concern. As with any doctrine, we must always go back to the Word of God as our standard. I would call the cross of Christ, not eschatology, the center. And further, I would argue that we must take our ideas—even of the future—from the cross. But Moltmann was correct in stressing that hope is important for living well now. To have hope is to look at the future optimistically. So, to some extent a person must have hope to live. People who despair do not go on.

During my pastoral life, there have been moments—upon hearing the stories or cries of congregants—that would leave me questioning the benefit of hope. "What can one truly hope for in this situation?" I can share personally that not only situations that those you know encounter rob you of hope like a towering bully demanding your lunch money, but even what people have seen me go through personally causes them to surrender hope. Questions have been spoken that are similar to this: "If my pastor has gone through this, and look how it ended for him, why should I have hope for anything different?"

How can any person remain sane in the midst of a tragic and desperate world in which we live? The senseless can, because they do not think about the future at all. Thinking people, who look at the pattern of the degradation of society, find the future grim. I've said it often: "My children and grandchildren will never know the America I once knew." Yet, in the spirit of one of my great heroes—Winston Churchill, who was a statesman and orator—made a mantra of the words *"never give up"* to the British during wartime in the 20th century.

This book is a personal perspective on where our hope comes from, even in the face of life challenges. The Christian life has its fill of suffering, setbacks, doubts, fears, tragedies, and confusion. What I have learned and surely know is that God gives us hope. Not only does the gospel of the Lord Jesus Christ give us Good News–that our sins are forgiven, and we can obtain eternal life–this same gospel inspires hope.

INTRODUCTION

Romans 15:4 *(NIV) says, "For everything that was written in the past was written to teach us, so that through endurance and the encouragement of the Scriptures we might have hope."*

Notice: the way to that sound and steadfast hope is through the Bible.

There are many versions of *The Wizard of Oz* now. All are supposedly based on The Wonderful Wizard of Oz[2], a 1900 children's novel written by American author L. Frank Baum. Since its first publication in 1900, it has been adapted many times for film, television, and theatre. The one that I saw first—which is the story's best-known adaptation and the version about which most cultural references to the story are based—was the one starring Judy Garland as Dorothy, produced in 1939.

You may recall Dorothy and her friends—the Scarecrow, the Tin Man, and the Cowardly Lion—are told to follow a yellow brick road to find their future. At the end of that yellow brick road would be their future; that is, the Wizard in Oz.

Likewise, the Cross, followed by the exhortation in Romans 15:4, gives us a road to hope. That begins with our trust in Jesus and His atoning sacrifice at Calvary, which initiates our journey marked with teaching, patient endurance, and encouragement. That is our yellow brick road—not to a Wizard of Oz, but to hope from the God of Heaven.

Let's walk that road.

The Teaching of the Scriptures

The first of the important steps along this road leading to hope is teaching, because it is through the teaching of the Scriptures that the other elements—endurance and encouragement—come. Christianity is a teaching faith, and our text is the Bible.

The Bible is from God. When Paul says that everything written in the past "was written to teach us," he did so intending that the church in future ages might be blessed by the writings of Moses and the psalms of David, so that we might profit by them. Paul's point is that God caused the human writers of the Bible to write as they did, because what He had in mind was the edification and encouragement of His people through the ages.

Other books may instruct and even inspire wonderfully, but only the Bible gives us a sure ground for hope, since only it speaks with full authority and trustworthiness about what God did to save us from sin and give us eternal life.

Patient Endurance

The second step on the road leading to hope is endurance, which some versions of the Scriptures translate to *patience* (King James Version), *perseverance* (New American Standard Bible) or even *patient endurance.* This word *(hypomonê)* occurs thirty-two times in the New Testament—sixteen times in Paul's writings, six of which are in Romans. The word involves both passively accepting what we cannot change and actively pressing on in faithful obedience and discipleship.

Hebrews 12:1–2

> *"Therefore, since we are surrounded by so great a cloud of witnesses, let us also lay aside every weight, and sin which clings so closely, and let us run with endurance the race that is set before us, looking to Jesus, the founder and perfecter of our faith, who for the joy that was set before him endured the cross, despising the shame, and is seated at the right hand of the throne of God."*

Our Christian journey is often referred to as a "walk"—and rightly so (Romans 6:4; 13:13; 2 Cor. 5:7; Gal. 5:16; Eph. 5:15; Col. 3:7; 1 Thess. 4:1, 12). However, the writer of Hebrews indicates it is a run, and one that is to require endurance. The description is the characteristic of a man who is not swayed from his deliberate purpose and his loyalty to faith by even the greatest trials and sufferings.

INTRODUCTION

Hebrews 10:36 (ESV)

"For you have need of endurance, so that when you have done the will of God you may receive what is promised."

This endurance implies hard labor. It implies carrying a burden faithfully. It implies the mission of what it means to be a Christian. It implies not quitting, or giving up, or giving in to the onslaught of the enemy's assault. Suffering you will face. Challenges will come. Opposition will stack up against you. But you are in a race to finish. And, more importantly, you are not without hope.

Encouragement

It is here where we make the third step on the road leading to hope: *"Let us run with endurance the race that is set before us,* **looking to Jesus, the founder and perfecter of our faith, who for the joy that was set before him** *endured the cross, despising the shame, and is seated at the right hand of the throne of God."*

We look to Jesus Christ. Why does this lead to hope? Because Jesus endured—even the suffering of the cross—yet His journey was rewarded with a place at the right hand of the throne of God. So we look to Him in the midst of our personal struggles. That is the way to run the race. As a runner focuses his eyes on the prize—perhaps, at the end of the race or the finishing mark—so we are to hold Jesus up before us. And as we run we keep our eye on Him, swerving not to the right or to the left, looking to Him for strength and grace and endurance—and in hope!

We are encouraged because we look to Jesus. He is the author of your faith. He is the pioneer of it, the one who went before you. He is the one who planted hope in you. He is author and finisher—the perfecter—of your faith.

The end result of this is hope. Paul, then, in Romans 15:4, would be saying that it is through our own personal enduring, as well as through the encouragement that we have in studying the Bible, that we find hope. In the text, the article is present before the word hope ("the hope"), meaning the

Christian hope. This is not just optimism that Paul is writing about—not a hope founded on something the world thinks possible. Also, the verb have is in the present tense, meaning that hope is a present possession.

The Biblical Meaning of Hope

Many of us have hopes every single day. When we speak of hope today, however, the word *hope* implies that there is doubt that what we hope for will actually happen.

This is not true in Biblical language. The word used for *hope* in the Bible contains no doubt that the hoped-for event will happen. The word for *hope* in Biblical Greek is ἐλπίς, pronounced *elpis*. This word would be translated today as *anticipation, expectation, or even confident expectation. Elpis* implies that something is going to happen, and the subject is anticipating it with confidence. Therefore, whenever you read the word *hope* in the New Testament, you should read that verse understanding *hope* to mean **confident expectation.**

There are over 50 uses of this word elpis, or "certain hope" in the New Testament. Here are a few uses in which confident expectation can replace the Greek word derived from *elpis*:

2 Corinthians 3:12

"Therefore, since we have such hope [confident expectation], we are very bold."

Romans 15:13

"May the God of hope [confident expectation], fill you with all joy and peace as you trust in Him, so that you may overflow with confident expectation by the power of the Holy Spirit."

Titus 1:2

"This truth gives them hope [confident expectation] that they have eternal life, which God -- who does not lie -- promised them before the world began."

1 Peter 3:15

"Always be prepared to give an answer to everyone who asks you to give the reason for the hope [confident expectation] that you have."

And finally, a personal favorite:

Hebrews 6:19

"We have this hope [confident expectation] as an anchor for the soul, firm and secure."

Truly, the Word of the Lord, and the patient endurance, and the encouragement that comes from Christ—who endured the cross—is the same that will give you hope. Your life can be anchored in hope.

The Cross

When Paul quotes Isaiah 11:10 in Romans 15:12, saying that *"the Gentiles will hope in him [that is, in Christ],"* he is thinking of personal salvation, of course. Any hope that does not lead to personal salvation results in what Paul said: *"If our hope in Christ is only in this life, we are more to be pitied than anyone in the world"* (1 Corinthians 15:19, NLT).

Paul's phrase describing the Ephesians before they came to Christ was *"without hope and without God in the world"* (Eph. 2:12). For the many who do not want God, they will be discovering that to be without God also means to be without hope.

We must remind everyone that where there is God, there is hope—and that Jesus Christ is still what Martin Luther called *der Heiden Heiland,* "the Savior [and, therefore, the hope] of the Gentiles."

INTRODUCTION

We live in a broken world. At some point, pain and suffering will crash into our lives. It's not a matter of if, but when. And when it does, we can be caught in the trap of believing, *"I am helpless. This is hopeless. There's no way out."*

But in **Romans 5:8** Paul tells us that hope in suffering is possible. *"While we were still sinners, Christ died for us."* Christ's death is a reminder of His overwhelming love for us. If Jesus was willing to die for us while we were in rebellion against Him, how much more will He care for us—His children—when tragedy strikes?

It's a hope that is anchored in the cross.

The cross also reveals that Jesus can identify with our pain. In hardship, He knows what we are feeling because He has experienced it Himself. He knows the pain of being betrayed by a close friend. He's experienced the humiliation of being falsely accused of something He didn't do. Jesus endured physical pain that felt like it would never end. The agony on the cross caused him to cry out the despair of abandonment.

Though He can empathize with our suffering, it doesn't mean all our pain will magically disappear, nor is there a lessening of the grief and sorrow that we are all bound to experience. Yet, the cross proves to us that a greater plan of God for us is at work.

What is that greater work? **The resurrection!** The reason we can have hope in suffering is because, with Jesus, death leads to new life. Therefore, we can be assured that our pain isn't wasted. Jesus is with us in the midst of it, and it inexplicably is leading to a greater good, and glory.

The cross is hopeful because a resurrection is inevitable. The shift from death to life not only fuels our hope—it's also the seedbed of joy.

Hope that provides joy in the midst of suffering isn't phony or fabricated happiness that's disconnected from the reality of one's circumstance. Rather, it's a deep-seated conviction that assures me—as we would say it in the church I grew up in—*"'E'rything gonna' be a'right!"* It comes from the assurance that

INTRODUCTION

Jesus is Lord of all. It's grounded in the hope of the larger story of God making all things new (Revelation 21:5).

While suffering can knock us down and cause a great sense of defeat, the cross and resurrection empower us to get back up and face another day. While pain and hardship, over time, can cause us to grow angry and bitter, focusing on Jesus and the victory He has secured can help us remain hopeful and full of joy. Nobody wants to suffer, but if we stay connected to Christ, He'll redeem our suffering in unexpected and brilliant ways.

The cross is the ultimate symbol of hope for all who believe. It is the place where our sins were atoned for and where our salvation was won. It is the place where Christ showed us the depths of His love and the extent to which He was willing to go to bring us to a place of rest in God.

Finally, the cross also gives us hope for our future. It is this message of hope that I share with you in the pages of this book. This is the hope that we have as we fix our eyes on Jesus. We have the hope of eternal life with Him—where there will be no more tears, no more pain, and no more suffering. We have the hope of being with Him forever in glory.

It is a *"Hope In Front of Me"* that I deeply desire to be in front of you. The words I share are experiences of mine, that may not be yours. My life has landed me in dark places—not as much physically as emotionally and mentally. Dare I say, even, spiritually.

There is a light, however. A light that can be seen. A light that is greater than any darkness. **Discover it. See it. Hope will arise.**

Let us fix our eyes on Jesus and find hope in the cross. Let us live our lives in the light of the hope that we have in Him, sharing His love and His grace with those around us.

1

REDISCOVERING HOPE

FINDING LIGHT IN LIFE'S DARKEST SEASONS

> "I've been running through rain that I thought would never end."
>
> —Danny Gokey, *Hope In Front of Me*

> "Why are you cast down, O my soul, and why are you in turmoil within me? Hope in God; for I shall again praise him, my salvation."
>
> —Psalm 42:5 (ESV)

At the time of writing this chapter we are approaching Advent. The Christmas season is upon us, and I am grateful. Christmas can be a reset: a chance to pause after a year of upheaval, unexpected tragedy, or the untimely death of a loved one. These seasons of failure and disappointment find new meaning in the light of Advent.

CHAPTER 1

For all of us in America, in the year of 2024, it is the end of an election—which causes more anxiety, angst, and stress than any American Christian should allow themselves to go through. In any event, Christmas does—or should I say, should—bring cheer, joy, and hope.

The end of this year echoes with memories of another significant moment: 2020. That unprecedented time touched every human life, as COVID-19 rewrote our understanding of "normal." Not one human being living in 2020 escaped the effects of this global pandemic.

The year 2020 began for us pastors with what seemed a clear calling. Looking back at 2020, we truly lived the truth of Paul's words in 1 Corinthians 2:9: *"No eye has seen, no ear has heard, and no mind has imagined what God has prepared for those who love him."*

We had no idea what was planned—by God—for us all. It was a year that challenged every assumption and shook every foundation: global pandemic, economic recession, mass unemployment, political division, cultural upheaval, racial reckoning, record wildfires, powerful hurricanes, devastating floods, and an election that tested our national resolve.

Many personal struggles emerged from these wide-scale events, while others faced trials completely unrelated. What became clear as that year drew to a close was that, whatever form the challenges took, the realities of life proved heavy and humbling.

Today is no different. We have been aware of the darkness around us. Yet darkness has always been God's chosen backdrop for revealing light. Just as the first Christmas came in a time of oppression and uncertainty, our current struggles create the perfect context for rediscovering hope.

> *"Do not be afraid. I bring you good news that will cause great joy for all the people. Today in the town of David a Savior has been born to you; he is the Messiah, the Lord. This will be a sign to you: You will find a baby wrapped in cloths and lying in a manger."*

Suddenly a great company of the heavenly host appeared with the angel, praising God and saying, "Glory to God in the highest heaven, and on earth peace to those on whom his favor rests." **(Luke 2:10-14)**

This is the news of the arrival of Jesus—the Messiah, the Son of God—news that drives away fear, fills us with joy, and holds us in peace. It's news of the reality we are invited to step into and experience.

It gives us hope.

While Advent points us toward the return of the Lord, the Christmas season invites us into a journey of rediscovering hope, peace, joy, and love—beginning with Christ Himself being born. Wherever you are in your anxiety, uncertainty, or pain; wherever you are on your own spiritual journey; wherever you find yourself in the midst of stress—let me invite you into this rediscovery of Hope.

The Reason For Hope

Rediscover Hope To Carry On

He gives strength to the weary and increases the power of the weak. Even youths grow tired and weary, and young men stumble and fall; but those who hope in the Lord will renew their strength. They will soar on wings like eagles; they will run and not grow weary, they will walk and not be faint.

—Isaiah 40:29-31

Those who hope in the Lord will:

1. renew their strength,
2. soar on wings like eagles,
3. run and not grow weary,
4. walk and not be faint.

CHAPTER 1

THOSE who put hope in the LORD!

Rediscover Hope That Sustains You

> "This hope will not disappoint us, because God's love has been poured out in our hearts through the Holy Spirit who was given to us."
> —**Romans 5:5 (CSB)**

There is an inseparable connection between God's received, understood, eternal love—and having hope. It has its properties of an inability to disappoint because it comes from the eternal Spirit of God, given to us in love.

It's part of the package when you are born again!

1 Peter 1:3

> "Celebrate with praises the God and Father of our Lord Jesus Christ, who has shown us his extravagant mercy. For his fountain of mercy has given us a new life—we are reborn to experience a living, energetic hope through the resurrection of Jesus Christ from the dead."

Rediscover Hope That Sees Beyond

Romans 8:22-26 (CSB)

> "For we know that the whole creation has been groaning together with labor pains until now. Not only that, but we ourselves who have the Spirit as the firstfruits—we also groan within ourselves, eagerly waiting for adoption, the redemption of our bodies. Now in this hope we were saved, but hope that is seen is not hope, because who hopes for what he sees? Now if we hope for what we do not see, we eagerly wait for it with patience. In the same way the Spirit also helps us in our weakness, because we do not know what to pray for as we should, but the Spirit himself intercedes for us with inexpressible groanings."

What is this saying? **We groan in hope.**

Our groaning *now* is leading to life then. We live everyday knowing that we have been adopted by God to be His children forever. That means that this body—which is not eternal—will fold up, and dissolve, yet our soul will live on forever.

We are redeemed!

It is this hope that helps us see *beyond* the depression of today; the despair of today; the discouragement of today.

Yes, the body may feel it. The mind may get a shot of torment. The heart may get heavy. The despair tries to set in.

But wait a minute!

It is a wall of *Hope!*

Hope says, *"You can't take my mind, sabotage my emotions, or rob me of peace, joy and happiness!"*

I don't see how all this will work out, but I have *patience in what I cannot see...*

Whether you are a Christ-follower or not, I can tell you that the God of Heaven has an end goal for you:

Romans 15:13 (ESV)

"May the God of hope fill you with all joy and peace in believing, so that by the power of the Holy Spirit you may abound in hope."

Let's learn from a psalmist about the condition we can all find ourselves in, where our hope comes from, and how we can rediscover it.

Notice these honest expressions in **Psalm 42:**

- **Verse 3:** "My tears have been my food day and night."
- **Verse 5:** "My soul is dejected and in such turmoil."

- **Verse 6:** "I am deeply depressed."

What caused such deep discouragement?

We are all depressed at times. We get down in the dumps. We sing the blues. We feel like God has forgotten us—and that we will never be able to get back on track with God again. It is a condition the old mystics accurately labeled "the dark night of the soul."

It is a puzzling condition too, especially for Christians. We identify with Erma Bombeck, who asks in the title of one of her best-selling books, *If Life Is a Bowl of Cherries, Why Am I Living in the Pits*[3]?

The psalmist tells us several key causes of his deep trouble. Though we don't know his identity beyond being one of the Sons of Korah, we can learn from the struggles he identifies:

First, he was experiencing a forced absence from the temple of God, where God was worshiped.

Psalm 42:1-2 (ESV)

"As a deer pants for flowing streams, so pants my soul for you, O God. My soul thirsts for God, for the living God. When shall I come and appear before God?"

He was far from Jerusalem and its temple worship on Mount Zion. Therefore, he felt himself to be cut off from God. The psalm begins with his panting after God *"as the deer pants for streams of water,"* when he cannot find it. He is far from home and feels that he is also far from God.

It is not that he does not believe that God is everywhere, or that God is not with him. But his being away from home has gotten him down, and his depressed state has caused him to feel that God is absent. The psalmist has expressed what we now know to be true: the more you attend worship gatherings, the better your mental health.

Americans' latest assessment of their mental health is worse than it's been at any point in the last two decades. While a majority of adults continue to rate their mental health as excellent (34 percent) or good (42 percent), those numbers represent a significant decline. The research consistently shows one powerful factor in maintaining mental health: regular worship attendance. Those who attend religious services weekly showed remarkable resilience, even during the challenges of recent years.

The location of the church I pastor is across from a large military base. Many from the military community call our church home. Worship gatherings in which they encounter the reality and presence of God is an escape—or at the very least, a relief—from the daily grind of briefings and maneuvers to protect our land and citizens from seen and unseen enemies.

Where this becomes relevant in regard to the testimony of King David in Psalm 42 is that, the often deployments away from home and places abroad—including field locations for months at a time—that experience is limited. There are chaplains assigned on most occasions, but the gatherings are limited or under restricted conditions. In any case, what they often share when home is their spiritual well-being was compromised simply to the lack of open, often, worship in which the presence of the Lord was pursued.

As I was writing this chapter, one couple in the military contacted me to say that they had not yet connected with a church that they call "home." Because of that, they seem so far from the place of spiritual nourishment, the Presence of God, and enriching fellowship. It is not that Church For The City is an end-all in their relational pursuit of God, but it is the place where they experienced what they are missing now.

Along with that are those in the agriculture community who work in Yuma for six months, and then in Colorado or the Salinas, CA valley for six months. Also, many in the medical community here are committed to traveling to other hospitals for months at a time. Eventually, they will leave Yuma, and subsequently, Church For The City. We have families in Japan, Washington, D.C., Texas, and so many more. It is more common than you may imagine. When you are away from your spiritual home, you feel like you have lost a spiritual connection.

Why It Matters:

Over the past 20 years, social-science research has continued to show the benefit of religiosity on well-being and flourishing, including mental and physical health. As Tyler VanderWeele noted, if one could conceive of a single element to improve the physical and mental health of millions of Americans—at no personal cost—what value would our society place on it[4]?

Church attendance isn't merely about feeling better—it's about finding the relief that comes from aligning ourselves with ultimate reality. What we discover in worship is the fulfillment of life's purpose: to glorify God and enjoy Him forever. We don't go to church to feel happy; we go to church to seek the source of our happiness (Ps. 16:11).

Recently, I shared the story of one who was a frequent worshipper in the house of the Lord, who walked away in pursuit of happiness by other means. Part of her story was that she would stand in front of her congregation and declare that she knew God, Jesus Christ, the Holy Ghost, prayer, and miracles were all real. She knew the potency of believing—that she was eternally loved, that life made sense.

But her curiosity pulled her away from the church and toward a secular university, where she, along with her peers, worked to build a rich, fulfilling life outside of faith.

Testing secular ideas for how to live well, she worked hard and built a community. She volunteered, cared for people she loved, pursued wellness, paid for workout classes, went to therapy, and visited saunas. She also tried book clubs and running clubs.

And yet, nothing ever felt like the worship she grew up experiencing in the little chapel where she learned and practiced to worship God.

Second, there were the taunts of unbelievers.

Psalm 42:3,10 (ESV)

> *"My tears have been my food day and night, while they say to me all the day long, "Where is your God?"... As with a deadly wound in my bones, my adversaries taunt me, while they say to me all the day long, "Where is your God?" People are asking him, where is your God? That is a cause for deep depression. Where is God indeed? Why doesn't God seem to hear my cries? Why doesn't he intervene to change my circumstances?"*

Third, are memories of better days.

Psalm 42:4 (NLT)

> *"My heart is breaking as I remember how it used to be: I walked among the crowds of worshipers, leading a great procession to the house of God, singing for joy and giving thanks amid the sound of a great celebration!"*

The psalmist was also troubled by memories of better days. He remembers and speaks of "when." There is a proper use of memory in times of depression—remembering God's past acts as an encouragement to believe that he will act for us again.

Now, his memory was torture.

Fourth, the overwhelming trials of life.

Psalm 42:7 (NLT)

> *"I hear the tumult of the raging seas as your waves and surging tides sweep over me."*

A bit further on in this psalm, the writer speaks of the overwhelming trials of his life, referring to them as "waves and breakers" that have swept over him.

Though we don't know the specific nature of these trials, we can understand their crushing weight.

Finally, there was the presumed failure of God to act quickly on our behalf.

Psalm 42:9 (CSB)

"I will say to God, my rock, 'Why have you forgotten me? Why must I go about in sorrow because of the enemy's oppression?'"

This painful cry to God reminds us of Jesus' words from the cross, *"My God, my God, why have you forsaken me?"* (Matt. 27:46). It is not unusual for a depressed person to feel forsaken by God.

These are the psalmist's reasons. What are yours? What's causing your depression, discouragement, and despair? What is causing these tormenting mental thoughts?

It is okay to not be okay—but it is not okay to stay there!

We are people who have a God who loves us, who cares for us, who desires to help us move from this place to that place.

We need the main ingredient: **Hope!**

How did the psalmist rediscover hope? He surrendered the season of life to the One who held all the resolve and the power to bring him to a healthy place.

Here it is:

Psalm 42:11 (CSB)

"Why, my soul, are you so dejected? Why are you in such turmoil? Put your hope in God, for I will still praise him, my Savior and my God."

It is okay to recognize the struggles of life. It is real. Daily—and particularly intense—personal challenges will cover your spiritual eyes from the hope before you.

If you can, look up like David and rejoice in the God of your salvation.

Hope will be rediscovered.

Practical Application

For those seeking to rediscover hope in life's darkest seasons:

1. **Turn to Scripture for encouragement.** As Romans 15:4 reminds us, "Through endurance and the encouragement of the Scriptures we might have hope." Make Bible reading and meditation a daily practice, especially during difficult times.

2. **Prioritize worship and community.** The research is clear - regular worship attendance significantly improves mental health and resilience. Don't isolate yourself when you're struggling; connect with your faith community.

3. **Practice the discipline of praise.** Like the psalmist in Psalm 42:11, choose to praise God even when your soul feels cast down. Say with him: "Put your hope in God, for I will still praise him, my Savior and my God."

4. **Remember God's faithfulness.** Look back at how God has carried you through previous difficulties. His track record of faithfulness in your past gives you reason to hope in your present situation.

Reflection Questions:

1. When have you experienced God's faithfulness during a particularly dark season of your life?

2. How has regular worship and fellowship with other believers strengthened your hope during difficult times?

3. What specific promises from Scripture have anchored your soul when circumstances seemed hopeless?

4. In what ways can you actively choose praise and gratitude even when your emotions don't match your circumstances?

Scripture References for Further Study:

- Psalm 42:5-11
- Romans 15:4
- Isaiah 40:29-31
- Romans 5:3-5
- 1 Peter 1:3-9
- Hebrews 6:19
- Jeremiah 29:11
- Lamentations 3:22-23

2

THERE'S A LIGHT

FINDING GOD'S PRESENCE IN LIFE'S DARKEST MOMENTS

"There's a light, I still see it."
—Danny Gokey, *Hope In Front of Me*

In September 1996, I arrived in Junction City, Oregon—a quaint town of fewer than 4,000 souls northeast of Eugene. Though I was one of the only Black residents in this predominantly Scandinavian community, what truly set me apart wasn't my race but my mission: seeking restoration after a spiritual fall.

What brought me to Junction City that late September evening was the aftermath of choices that had wounded my family and church. Emotional affairs—often dismissed as less significant than physical infidelity—can be equally devastating in their impact on relationships and spiritual well-being.

Through a pastor in Yuma, I was connected to Pastor Jon Bowers of Christ's Center in Junction City. Over a landline phone conversation, Pastor

CHAPTER 2

Jon's words carried an assurance of understanding and love for broken pastors. He believed the School of Restoration, now called Restoration Ministries, could be God's instrument for rebuilding my relationship with Christ.

With that hope, I made the drive on September 17, 1996.

The evening of September 19th, I pulled into Junction City in a white Hyundai Sonata. The autumn air was crisp, and darkness had already settled over the unfamiliar streets. I knew no one except for a voice on the phone, had no guaranteed place to stay, and carried no certainty of whether I could ever return to my family and church. The darkness wasn't just in the sky—it had settled into my fears, my uncertainties, and seemingly my very soul.

To my surprise, settling into the town and church proved delightful. The ministry school began transforming my life, and friendships formed naturally. Some of those bonds remain unbroken nearly three decades later. As I write this, I'm anticipating a visit from Mike and Terryl Kaiser, dear friends from that season.

Another treasured friendship was with Richard Guth, who shared my passion for sports but also had a gift for hospitality. One night that would prove pivotal began with Richard's simple invitation to watch *Monday Night Football*—the Oakland Raiders versus the Kansas City Chiefs. The promise of fried chicken and fellowship was irresistible, especially since I didn't have a television in my fifth-wheel home.

Living alone on remote property in Brownsville, Oregon—where my closest neighbor was actor Sam Elliott's 200-acre spread a couple miles down the hill—any invitation for company was welcome. In seven months, I glimpsed the famous actor only once. But on this particular evening, the twenty-six mile distance from church and friends, combined with the initial stages of what would become known as the Catastrophic Willamette Valley Floods of 1996, made me hesitate. Twenty-three inches of rain had already fallen in just days.

The invitation came on Sunday, December 8th. Rain had been constant, and the creeks near my residence were rising alongside the drainage ditches that lined the roads. By Monday the 9th, the downpour continued. Yet the appeal of football, fellowship, and fried chicken proved stronger than my weather concerns. Though I wondered about the rising waters during my time in Junction City, I made the drive. The Raiders' victory, warm fellowship, and perfect chicken (with a boxed portion for home) made it seem worthwhile.

The drive back to Brownsville was another matter entirely. Twenty-six miles of dark country roads stretched before me, including crossing the Willamette River between Junction City and Harrisburg. After Harrisburg came miles on Diamond Hill Road before crossing I-5 eastward into the hills.

Around 9pm, the sky was pitch black, the only illumination coming from occasional vehicles on I-5 visible from the overpass. Something unsettling crept over me. My emotions began to fracture, my mind constricting as if caught in a steel trap.

Too late, I began questioning whether the evening's pleasures were worth what was coming.

Then it happened.

Just past the interstate, as I cruised downhill from the overpass, my headlights revealed what looked like a pond stretching across Diamond Hill Road (which becomes Gap Road leading into Brownsville). The drainage ditches had overflowed, sending water rushing across the asphalt. I had never driven through flooding before. I didn't know that my Sonata was about to hydroplane.

The loss of control was instantaneous. Terror swept through me as the car slid sideways. By the time it stopped, I knew I'd left the asphalt far behind. But where had I ended up? In the darkness, I had no idea.

My heart hammered against my ribs. My hands shook on the steering wheel. I tried to steady my breathing, grateful to be alive and apparently unharmed. The car seemed intact. But that moment of relief was short-lived.

Then I felt it: a slight shift beneath the wheels. The Sonata was moving, but not forward—downward. Ice-cold winter water began seeping under the

CHAPTER 2

doors. In that moment, I realized where I was: perched atop a drainage ditch, and my car was slowly sinking into it.

Fear froze me. How far had I slid from the road? What should I do?

I pushed against the door, fighting the water's pressure. When it finally opened, a rush of freezing water poured in. The water felt like ice against my skin. My lungs tightened with each breath as panic threatened to overtake me. I couldn't stay in the sinking car—but in the pitch darkness, the freezing water, and my body feeling like it was going into a hypothermic shock, every option seemed dangerous.

Then came a moment that illuminated far more than just my physical circumstances. About fifteen yards to my left, as I sat in the driver's seat sinking into despair, I saw lights—tail lights, headlights, and what appeared to be light from an open door.

Even in my terror, the Spirit of the Lord revealed something profound: those lights pierced the darkness like a beacon of *hope*! Yes, hope for rescue from the floodwaters—but even more, from the darkness that had flooded my life.

In God's Providence, He was speaking. Though far from an ideal situation, I was sitting exactly where God's sovereignty had been designed for a greater purpose. Those lights before me became the hope that would lift me from both the darkness of my circumstances and the car I was sinking in.

Determined to reach that light, I gathered what belongings I could under one arm and braced myself to exit the car. I blindly threw my things toward where I thought the road might be. As I stepped out, the true peril of my situation became clear—my foot found no ground. For over six feet there was nothing but water. At 6'1½" tall, my head went completely under.

Hypothermia seized my body instantly, and the fear of death gripped my heart and mind—again. I was cold, surrounded by darkness, and terrified.

But I had *hope*.

Why? How? Because of those lights! Above my head, thirty yards away, a vehicle's lights pierced the darkness.

Here's what you need to know: I had no idea who was in that vehicle, what kind it was, or who was driving. It could have been someone who recognized my car—or it might have been someone seeing an easy target for harm.

At that moment, none of those possibilities mattered. There was only one objective: *get to those lights.*

That was my hope.

You may not have faced literal floodwaters, but many of you reading this now have experienced moments when everything seemed to be sinking. In those moments we all desperately search for *light.*

We are drawn to light because it gives us hope. The light was bringing hope to my insecurity, fear of being unsafe, and feeling of uncertainty.

That is what light does.

In cold, dark, fearful places—in places of pain and abuse, in the dreads of addiction, sin, and the weight of traumatic experiences—we have a hope.

That hope is the **light of the world.**

John 1:4–5 (ESV)

"In him was life, and the life was the light of men. The light shines in the darkness, and the darkness has not overcome it."

This great image—the image of Christ—is the *light of the world.* Here we read, *"In him was life, and that life was the light of men. The light shines in the darkness, but the darkness has not understood it."* Later, Jesus declares pointedly, *"I am the light of the world"* (8:12).

Several years ago, an old woman in the bush country of southern Rhodesia shared a profound truth with a missionary: *"You have brought us the light, but we don't seem to want it. You have brought us the light, but we still walk in darkness."*

Though she spoke of her African community, her words capture humanity's universal response to Jesus Christ when He first shone upon the world. He was the light of the world. In one sense He had *always* been the light of the world. Yet, when He appeared, the world rejected Him—because it preferred darkness.

What does John mean when he declares that Jesus Christ is the *light of men?* Light universally represents illumination—whether of mind, heart, or space.

Before Christ came, the world lay in darkness, not knowing God. When Christ came, His light shone before men, revealing the knowledge of God in Jesus' face.

The Creator never intended for humanity to live in darkness or hopelessness. Paul makes this clear in **Ephesians 2:12:** *"You lived in this world without God and without hope."*

Having no hope is synonymous with living without God. There can be no hope when there is no God. Yet when *the Light* shines through, not only can we have hope—we can have God Himself.

Consider the significance of light and hope throughout Scripture:

Psalm 27:1

"The Lord is my light and my salvation."

Psalm 36:9

"For with you is the fountain of life; in your light we see light."

Psalm 104:1-2

"Praise the Lord, O my soul. O Lord my God, you are very great; you are clothed with splendor and majesty. He wraps himself in light as with a garment; he stretches out the heavens like a tent."

1 John 1:5

"God is light; in him there is no darkness at all."

God is light!

We recognize this truth personally every time we sing some of our most beautiful hymns:

Eternal light! Eternal light!
How pure the soul must be
When, placed within Thy searching light,
It shrinks not, but with calm delight
Can live, and look on Thee! [5]

For decades hymns, have comforted many Christian pilgrims, sojourning through life, facing peril and tragedy. As a pastor, I often weave hymns in my sermons. The words bring peace during our darkest hours. When presiding over a funeral or at the bedside of a dying loved one, grieving families can—for just a moment—stand in the perfect light from God above.

Consider this one by Walter Chalmers Smith:

Immortal, invisible, God only wise,
In light inaccessible hid from our eyes,
Most blessed, most glorious, the Ancient of Days,
Almighty, victorious, Thy great name we praise. [6]

The work of a pastor is not to solve people's problems. We really cannot do that. And we certainly cannot be "God" to them. We are *hope* givers, who point people to the light.

CHAPTER 2

In thirty-two years of leading a congregation, the situations people have shared with me—that they have found themselves in—are innumerable. People of all walks of life; that is, the wealthy and successful, the less fortunate and down and out. The social class and status may be different, but despair has no respect for people.

In that darkness, the need is the same: *it is the light of Christ!* Only when they encounter Christ does the darkness recede.

E. M. Blaiklock, former professor of classics at Auckland University in New Zealand, makes these observations:

"God is light. The image is satisfyingly complete. Light penetrates the unimaginable depths of space, far beyond the limits of human vision... Without light there is no vision, no view of reality, no confident journeying, no growth save of chill and evil things, no health, no life. The hand shrinks from the cold and slimy life which survives sluggishly in dark caves... But light, like God, exists by itself, apart from that which it illuminates."[7]

The image is rich and totally appropriate to describe the Lord Jesus Christ. God the Father is light. So also is Christ the Son. He is the image of the invisible God, the One who fills all in all. In Him we see and know the Father.

By His coming into the world, Jesus exposed the works of darkness—even where men thought they had most light. As the woman in Africa noted, many still do not want it. You can reject Christ's light, as many have done. You can try to remove His presence from your life.

But as John implies, *the darkness did not overcome the light.*

Or you can do what God desires.

What gives hope such promise is that the light of Jesus Christ has never been overcome by darkness. In fact, John tells us, *"The light still shines in the darkness, and the darkness has never put it out."*

Spiritual darkness tried to eclipse the True Light, Jesus Christ—but He simply overcame it.

Malcolm Muggeridge, England's well-known satirist and social critic who journeyed from skepticism to faith, expressed it powerfully:

"Having seen this other light [the light of God revealed in Jesus Christ], I turn to it, striving and growing toward it as plants do toward the sun.... Though, in terms of history, the darkness falls, blacking out us and our world, You have overcome history. You came as light into the world in order that whoever believes in You should not remain in darkness. Your light shines in the darkness, and the darkness has not overcome it. Nor ever will."[8]

On one occasion in the early years of my ministry, I was studying late into the night at the church. As I was leaving, a man was walking by the church. It was actually early in the morning—*dark-thirty,* as it is often called. It seemed odd for him to be walking alone at the time.

I called out to him to ask if everything was okay. *"Do you need anything?"*

He walked closer to me and honestly I got a bit concerned. He looked very troubled. I wasn't sure if it was despair or evil. Trying to still my posture, he said, *"It is not good. I am not good. Are you a Father?"* a reference from the Catholic faith, of course.

There was no time to distinguish, so I said, *"Yes.."*

"Can you pray for me?" he asked.

In faith (and somewhat trepidation), I prayed fervently and passionately, asking the Lord to help him, heal him, and deliver him. I didn't know his name, and never asked him what it was. He never asked me about mine. All I can recall, these many years later, is his response when I finished praying:

"Whoa! Wow! You did it, man! I can see the light! The darkness is gone! I can see the light!"

After those words, he turned and walked away. I've never seen him again.

But I remember the effect: **the Light has come, and darkness cannot ever overcome it!**

Practical Application

For those seeking light in their darkness:

1. **Turn toward the light.** Just as my survival depended on moving toward those distant headlights, our spiritual life depends on actively turning toward Christ's light. Even when we can't see the path clearly, we must move toward His light.

2. **Trust the light's guidance.** The journey through darkness requires faith that the light will lead us to safety. Christ's light never fails, even when we can't see where each step leads.

3. **Reflect the light.** Once we've found our way to the light, we become bearers of that same hope for others still trapped in darkness.

Reflection Questions:

1. **When have you experienced a moment of light breaking through your darkness?** How did it change your perspective?

2. **How do you distinguish between false lights that might lead you astray and the true Light of Christ?**

3. **In what ways can your story of finding light in darkness help others on their journey?**

4. **Consider how physical darkness and spiritual darkness parallel each other.** What lessons from one help you understand the other?

The Light Still Shines

Remember this truth: No matter how deep the waters, how dark the night, or how hopeless the circumstance—**there's a light.**

That light is **Jesus Christ,** and **He still shines.**

He overcame darkness at the cross.

He overcomes darkness in our lives today.

And He will overcome all darkness in the end.

Just as those distant headlights gave me hope on that flooded road in Oregon, Christ's light offers hope in every darkness we face.

The question isn't whether the light shines—it's whether we'll turn toward it.

Scripture References for Further Study:

- Isaiah 9:2
- John 8:12
- 2 Corinthians 4:6
- 1 Peter 2:9
- Revelation 21:23
- Psalm 119:105

3

EYES ENLIGHTENED

DISCOVERING GOD'S PURPOSE THROUGH LIFE'S SEASONS

What I want to do in this chapter is help you understand that the acts and ways of God in our life—at any age and season He determines—point us to knowing Him better. Through this knowing, He enlightens the eyes of our heart to the hope of our calling.

I say this is the purpose of this chapter—and that it is. The reason being that it reflects the prayer of the Apostle Paul—a prayer that has become mine for you and anyone who reads this book. Here are the words of the Apostle:

Ephesians 1:17-18 (CSB)

"I pray that the God of our Lord Jesus Christ, the glorious Father, would give you the Spirit of wisdom and revelation in the knowledge of him.

CHAPTER 3

I pray that the eyes of your heart may be enlightened so that you may know what is the hope of his calling..."

Living on Berkshire Terrace in Hampton, Virginia marked a pivotal time in my life. The home was very nice, as was the neighborhood. Of all places I lived with my stepdad and my mom during those few years on the East Coast, I enjoyed this home most of all.

It was here I viewed the Bicentennial Celebration for our great nation. I also recall watching the Portland Trail Blazers win the NBA championship led by Bill Walton, Maurice Lucas, and Lionel Hollins. They upset my beloved Philadelphia 76ers—an unbelievable outcome given the 76ers' legendary lineup: Henry Bibby, Joe Bryant (Kobe's dad), Doug Collins, Darryl "Chocolate Thunder" Dawkins, World B. Free, George McGinnis, Mike Dunleavy, and the greatest of all, Julius "Dr J." Erving.

No way were they to lose. And yet, they did.

To add insult to injury, my beloved Los Angeles Dodgers lost the World Series to the New York *damn* Yankees!

Sports was not going well for me personally, either. I was not a great athlete—maybe not even a good one. Yet desire, heart, and passion were certain.

Bethel High school was well known for its athletes—Allen Iverson, the NBA Hall of Famer, who was a standout at Bethel in basketball and football. Football at Bethel was *competitive!* If you were going to get playing time in a game or be considered valuable enough to be on the practice squad, you had to have what it took.

Though I got a few opportunities, they were not many. And I knew why. I wasn't good enough.

Outside of reading—particularly the Bible—playing a sport was my joy. But instead of football being fun and joyful, it was painful. Oftentimes, humiliating, as I tried to compete against athletes well above my ability.

Friends were not in abundance. The neighborhood was all white, except one Black family who lived across from us diagonally. Having white friends was not a concern for me. I had them in Yuma, AZ before moving east, and of course, I have many now. The church I pastor is over 50% white.

But folks, this is Virginia in 1977! Interracial relationships of any manner were not ignored—nor were they encouraged.

The Black family that lived across from us had a son my age. As our parents developed a relationship, it seemed right and expected that he and I would also. There was no reason for me not to. I wanted someone in my neighborhood to consider a friend and a hangout buddy.

Because most people at my high school were bused in, the chances of any of them becoming a friend was slim to none. I would walk to school. So my friends needed to come from my neighborhood. And it wasn't happening with the whites.

I was all in with building a relationship with Juaquin—until I witnessed behavior that was counter to my values.

Most of the time we would ride our bikes or spend time talking in Juaquin's bedroom or in the backyard. One particular day when I went over, Juaquin was in the backyard. As I arrived some of his behavior seemed odd. For whatever reason I didn't get too alarmed, but remained keenly observant.

It was when he went to a shed that was storage for lawn equipment —to sniff gas and paint—that the odd behavior was confirmed. **Strike one.**

A few days later, while visiting, we were having a conversation in Juaquin's bedroom. I am sure his parents were home, but that was not a factor. Somewhere in the conversation, Joaquin thought it appropriate to reveal his sexual identity issues—or at the least, his sexual experimentations. When he approached me in an inappropriate manner, it was offensive and appalling. **That was strike two.**

CHAPTER 3

At that time, I didn't have the temperament to react in a manner I might today. So with no action or reason given to anyone, I never spoke to him or spent another minute with him again.

Strike three would not have been good for him.

My parents—nor his—were never told why I was not going to spend time with Juaquin again. Yet this left me in a crisis. I didn't have any friends. Time was spent with my sister Donna and brother Eric, which was enjoyable. Yet a peer was missed. An emptiness or void was created.

In retrospect, the Lord used this to isolate me for what I now presume was His providence—for what He was preparing me to do according to His divine calling and purpose for my life.

There was a church mother, Helen Nevels, from my hometown and home church who would write to me. The letters were a joy to receive. Not only did they help me, to some degree, stay connected to "home," the many scriptures and words of encouragement assisted me in applying biblical principles to my life, during this season.

There was a wooded area near us that I would ride my bike to enter. From certain spots, one could see some ball games at an elementary school. Watching increased my yearning for community and friendships. At the same time, it was a place of prayer and talks with God.

Though I was only 13-14 years old, Bible reading, prayer and relationship with the Lord was a prominent part of my life.

My wife, Virginia, and I were in Hampton, Virginia a few years ago. I went to look for that wooded area so she could see the spot I often referred to when sharing certain monumental moments in my life.

Then it seemed so lonely. I felt so isolated from anything that had relevance to my life, or any connection with who I was—or who I thought I was. There were days those woods seemed like a wilderness.

And yet, without me knowing it, the Lord had me in that place—as He did the Children of Israel for forty years—not to get a hold of who I was, but rather, to learn who He is, and what He wanted to do in my life.

One afternoon in my spot in the woods, a thought came to me that remained with me until 1993. That thought was this: *"You were not made for this."*

I knew what that meant to me then, though I could not explain what I "knew" theologically—or even practically. It just made sense to me. I was not made for this loneliness and isolation. The purpose of my life was not to be lost with the acts of the ill-reputed friend, the aching separation from my hometown, and the lack of ability to do well at what I enjoyed (that is, football).

But what was I made for?

This chapter would be shorter if the answer to that one question had been resolved at the age of 14.

How I wish it was!

So many silly decisions, poor choices, and bad behavior would have been prevented. Nope! I wasn't smart enough to spare myself a few of life's unpleasantries.

Rather, stumbling in the dark—*hit and miss in life and ministry*—for nearly two decades is what my footprints evidenced.

Until I understood the purposes of what I experienced at 13 and 14 years of age—with a dramatic call to plant the church I pastor now: Church For The City, in Yuma, AZ.

Some 15 years later, I find myself alone again—isolated, and in a place to hear from the Lord—back in Yuma, married and raising three children.

A mentor who pastored a church in Dallas, TX, suggested that time with him at his church would be an opportunity to grow in the ministry and shape

CHAPTER 3

the call of God. That would require leaving my job at Pepsi-Cola and relocating my family.

Believing this was the will of God for me and my family, I resigned from my job, all the duties at my local church, and moved my family into a duplex we owned as we prepared to move. The date of arrival in Dallas was set for March 15th, 1993.

It was exciting for me to know that someone valued my gifting in the body of Christ—and also wanted to help me grow and develop in my call.

The move was a bit scary, honestly. Resettling my family and securing employment to provide for them was also a concern.

Yet none of that outweighed the excitement and hope in front of me.

As the days drew nearer to March 15th, so did the swell of thoughts and emotions.

Some days my head was full of thoughts that ranged from *uncertainty, to why is this necessary,* to what if this turns out to be a bad move?

I will be living in a place that was not my home, nor a choice made with research and perspective benefit. It was made because of my ambition—for my own good, not necessarily that of my family.

What if the relationship with my mentor goes south?

What if I don't like the church?

Or the church family and staff do not like the position I would be placed in?

There was a lot that added to the anxiety and the thoughts.

And still, all systems were go.

Until I realized—I hadn't heard from the one most important: **My Lord and my God.**

The day I called the pastor to let him know I was not coming was the beginning of a *return* to the wooded area.

Two to three weeks shy of March 15th, a season of loneliness and isolation reemerged—just as I remembered it before.

Thank the Lord, Pepsi-Cola allowed me to return to my job. We also found a home that needed a complete remodel after being abandoned for quite a few years. The home was cinderblock—so externally solid. The inside was a different story. Not to mention, the lot looked like typical Yuma desert land, with nothing but sand and tumbleweeds.

Even with that, and not knowing what the Lord wanted me to do or what He would speak into my life, I accepted that we were to remain in Yuma.

Without a church home now, I was leading studies with my family at home. Again, this added to the isolation. Being in the house of God and an active part of the local church was my life from birth. The only years it was not a central part of my life were those years of ages 13-14.

Same feeling.

Same season.

Replaying all over again.

The thought that caught my attention then comes back to me again: *"You are not made for this."*

If I only knew *for what!* Knowing it—I did know—meant knowing *Him* better. So the studies with my family, the prayers, and pressing in to Him was certainly the best place for me to pursue to know Him better.

Once the home was in livable condition, I began to assess what to do with the yard. The initial work was cleaning all the tumbleweeds, and hard-raking the land to somewhat level the sand and dirt.

One day, while considering how much seed and fertilizer to get grass growing, I turned on a water hose and just held it in my hand. Honestly, I don't

CHAPTER 3

know why now. It could've been to see the texture of dirt versus sand—or to see if the ground would hold water or just absorb it. I am not sure.

I do know that in the desert here, to grow grass you must prep the ground in some manner, spread grass seed, and fertilizer (primarily manure), to have a healthy lawn of grass.

God used this moment to finish the statement I had heard from Him in a couple of seasons: *"You were not made for this."*

As I held the water hose with an undefined purpose, I heard what I would defend as an audible voice that said:

"As sure as I raise up grass in this lawn, you will raise a church in this city."

I looked around to see who could be talking to me. There is no one in sight!

Now, this may be a good spot to bring you into my world.

The church I attended in Yuma, AZ was built by my grandfather. When people use the term *"pew baby,"* that was me! Except for the few years I lived in the eastern United States, I was in that church almost everyday of my life.

At this time, I am 29 years old. Though there were some years of not being in fellowship with Christ, my life was set apart to serve Him. The church I was raised in—and had just left, leaving my family churchless—was just as much a part of my lifetime plan as going to heaven.

Though I had a job, a home, and my family—my life was *turned upside down!* With all that I had, there was a great loss. My spiritual community life, and fellowship were in turmoil. I didn't know what to do. I didn't know what God wanted. And I wasn't hearing anything that made sense or gave me direction.

And then—this happens!

In my condition and state of mind, it seemed that I was really at a lower place than I had presumed. *I am hearing voices!*

Yet as I contemplate what was just said and what was happening, I heard it again:

"As sure as I raise up grass in this lawn, you will raise up a church in this city."

That time—I knew it was the Lord!

With that promise, and that hope, I watered the **dirt** each day for two weeks, adding no seeds and no fertilizer.

I watered the dirt each day on the **word of the Lord!**

In about ten days, all witnessed a full lawn of radiant grass—as if laid down, cultivated and manipulated for growth by the most skilled landscaper.

I knew then what I was born to do.

From six people in my living room, to a church over 2,000 today—and with my eyes enlightened—the *hope of my calling* is being lived out.

Prayer is an essential part of our relationship with God. It has been called one of the tools of Christian growth and one of the spiritual disciplines. Prayer is part of each Christian's life.

We have a desire, and we have a need. We have a request, and we should therefore bring it to God in prayer *(Phil. 4:6)*. God will help us in our need. If we are mindful of how great the task is, and how small our own abilities are, we'll find it easy to ask for help from the great Shepherd of our souls.

Prayer serves not only the people we are praying for—it also serves the person who prays.

Part of the normal format for a Greek letter was the thanksgiving section, and most of Paul's letters have this. Often it is just a prayer of thanks; sometimes it is also a request. Paul prayed about his churches, and he also prayed *for* his churches.

Paul does not hesitate to tell his readers that he is praying for them, nor is he reluctant to tell them what he is praying for. Paul's prayer of petition moves from the general to the specific:

Ephesians 1:17-19 (NLT)

"Asking God, the glorious Father of our Lord Jesus Christ, to give you spiritual wisdom and insight so that you might grow in your knowledge of God.

I pray that your hearts will be flooded with light so that you can understand the confident hope he has given to those he called—his holy people who are his rich and glorious inheritance.

I also pray that you will understand the incredible greatness of God's power for us who believe him."

In verse 17 he says that he is praying that God might give the Ephesians *"the Spirit of wisdom and revelation"* in order that they *"may know him better."* Then, in verses 18 and 19 he says that he is praying that *"the eyes of [their hearts] may be enlightened"* in order that they may know:

- *"the hope to which he has called [them],*
- *the riches of his glorious inheritance in the saints,*
- *and his incomparably great power for us who believe."*

Before speaking directly to you, let me share about another man in a tough place who, by God's providence, discovered exactly what God called him to do.

Barnabas appears in the New Testament, primarily in Acts and Paul's letters. In the Book of Acts, Barnabas played a key role in introducing Saul (later known as Paul) to the apostles in Jerusalem. Barnabas, having already believed in Saul's conversion, took him to the apostles, explained his transformation, and helped him gain acceptance within the early Christian community *(Acts 11)*.

Later, Barnabas also sought out Saul in Tarsus and brought him to Antioch, where they worked together to teach the church. From there, they traveled together, ministering the gospel of Christ, planting churches, and discipling converts.

After their first missionary journey, the two dear brothers had a dispute and separated *(Acts 15)*. Interestingly enough, we see much of what Paul did after that. But we don't see much of Barnabas—except these words:

"Barnabas took Mark with him and sailed away to Cyprus" (Acts 15:39).

You would have presumed that Barnabas life was upended—similar to mine. Separated from his spiritual community, and his purpose in life ends in turmoil. Yet, that is not the end of the story. This same Apostle Paul sends a message to Barnabas in Cyprus that he needed John Mark.

2 Timothy 4:11 (ESV)

"Luke alone is with me. Get Mark and bring him with you, for he is very useful to me for ministry."

> "Through his story of mentoring John Mark, we see how God enlightens the eyes of His servants to see their calling."

Barnabas served the Lord according to the Lord's purpose—and that was to mentor John Mark for ministry that would last beyond him and become worldwide as John Mark served with the great Apostle Paul. What am I saying? Through his story of mentoring John Mark, we see how God enlightens the eyes of His servants to see their calling.

What about for you? What is God calling you to do?

It was a wooded area for me. It was a noted ministry for Barnabas. Yours may be a different place, a different act, and a different approach to life. But there is purpose for you—designed by God, and set before you to discover.

I know that He will give wisdom and revelation to know, *as you know Him better.*

May I suggest:

- Ask the God of our Master, Jesus Christ, the God of glory—to give you a desire and persistence to pursue knowing Him. As you do, have your eyes clear and focused so that you can see exactly what it is He is calling you to do. Finally, grasp the immensity of this glorious way of life He has for you as His follower.

Practical Application

Reflection Questions:

1. When has God used seasons of isolation in your life to prepare you for His purposes?

2. How have you experienced the "eyes of your heart being enlightened"?

3. What might God be calling you to that seems as impossible as grass growing in desert sand?

4. How does knowing God better help you understand your calling?

Scripture References for Further Study:

- Ephesians 1:17-18
- Philippians 4:6
- Acts 4:36-37
- Acts 9:26-27
- 2 Timothy 4:11
- Colossians 4:10

4

THE GOD WHO IS THERE

FINDING HIS PRESENCE IN OUR DARKEST SEASONS

> *"There's a hand still holding me, even when I don't believe it"*
>
> —Danny Gokey, *Hope In Front of Me*

Years of difficulty ensued while I was separated from a wife of 23 years. Discovering traits and characteristics of my personality and carnal nature that youth and marriage had disguised were incomprehensible. Pain, hurt, shame and guilt led to a lengthy tunnel that kept going—with no evident door out, nor an end to the tunnel.

So, I kept going.

The lack of identity (or not knowing who you truly are) is not threatened by long, dark tunnels. You don't see anything—not even yourself. There is no light shining on you. Nothing to do but keep walking without any protest to what is not right.

CHAPTER 4

You don't stop, to keep from restraining the flow of others behind you. As long as you are in front and still moving forward, so will they.

And life goes on—having never stopped to see what the tunnel hid.

The analogy speaks of my life. Since this is not a memoir or autobiography, I will not go into much detail. What is relevant to this writing is how events in my life that seemed minuscule had an immense effect on my already damaged and distorted identity.

Recognition was one of the most redemptive revelations I could've received.

Buena Vista, Colorado is an outdoorsman's paradise. The trails and mountains beckon the heartened hiker; great fishing awaits for both sport and provision. Herds of deer walk into your yard like invited guests that stay past their welcome. The landscape is green and picturesque in spring, summer, and fall; a truly white Christmas graces winter. A great escape from the Arizona heat in summer. However, my reason for being there was not for an escape— rather, to be healed.

When I arrived there for two weeks of intensive counseling, it was January. The snow was enjoyable; the cold was more bearable than you would think a Yuma boy could handle (I'd lived in snow before.) The altitude was hard for me to get acclimated to. However, the most difficult encounter was facing a counselor who made me face myself—better said, made me see myself. I was out of the tunnel, and everything about me was made known.

Wil Franz was a Christian, who was charismatic and German. LOL! (Okay, maybe you have to experience a charismatic German to see the humor in it.) He has a unique personality that is perplexing, while still being brilliant! My inhibitions and protected persona made it difficult to receive from Wil, initially. Yet he wasn't set back by me in any manner. For three hours a day, Monday through Friday of week one, he chiseled at my shell while plumbing tributaries of truth into my heart. The realities of who I'd become were truly *shock and awe*, and how Wil pointed out my flaws was quite amazing.

To give you a glimpse of how our sessions would go, do your best to picture this:

During a particular hour, I am describing some events that had recently occurred at home in Yuma—events related to the reason I came for counseling. My suppressed passion begins to rise in the intensity of my voice. In the explanation, I am defending my feelings, attitude, and behavior. I am looking right at Wil, expressing myself with hand motions (to prove the validity of my statements, I am sure)…

And he just starts speaking in tongues—*with his eyes open, staring right at me*—with no conscious recognition of the rude interruption.

I stop.

Ask him what he is doing.

And he gets *louder*, staring at me!

After what seemed like an eternity of him speaking in tongues—at this annoying volume—looking at me like Norman Bates in *Psycho*, he begins to speak to the Lord in English.

It was only a few words:

"Lord, you tell him."

That's it! That is all he said.

And just as intense as Wil was rudely speaking in tongues, was a voice in my head—which I *know* was the Spirit of the Lord. While I am staring at Wil, wanting to be angry at him, the Lord is convincing me that *everything* I just went off about was indefensible, unjustified, and that *I* am the one that should be apologizing—instead of feeling validated for being angry at the people I was complaining about.

CHAPTER 4

There you have it. You now know why this was a unique and gifted individual—and why the Lord sovereignly worked it out for him to be *my* counselor.

At the age of 44, the abandonment, rejection, and neglect had surfaced in fear, insecurity and anger. To compensate for what was present—but unseen by me—was a deliberate intent to build an image that would not allow me, my family, and particularly my children, to lack anything.

The trigger?

An iPod.

Delivered to the office of the counseling center by a courier.

The latter part of week one, I made a few attempts to get a workout at a local gym. The first day was not successful. I struggled on the treadmill and also on the weight machines. I assumed it was not being acclimated. So I walked out of the *gym* after less than a half hour.

The second day was not much different. Yet I didn't want to think it was simply the altitude. There had to be something more. Accepting that the altitude was affecting a gym rat like me just didn't seem feasible.

But again, I walked out without much accomplished at all.

Day three... I figured it out.

When I came into the gym to start my regular routine—which began on the treadmill—I noticed that everyone had an iPod and earbuds. (There were no AirPods back then and Apple phones with all your music like there are now—just iPods.)

Then it hit me!

Of course I couldn't work out like everyone else—*I didn't have what everyone else had!*

It wasn't the altitude. It was the lack of equipment that allowed me to perform like everyone else.

So what do I do? I walked out of the gym and call Yuma. I told my son where my iPod was and asked him to overnight it to me.

Why should I be lacking and feeling less adequate than everyone else working out?

Day four.

I am in my session with Wil Franz when a knock on the office door brings in a small box for me.

Immediately, I knew what it was. I opened the box and celebrated—having my iPod.

I am complete.

No longer inadequate. No longer less than anyone else.

I have what they have, so I am what they are!

And I can do what they do!

The iPod proves it!

After observing my behavior upon receiving the package, Wil asked me why I had that sent to me.

Without thinking I said, *"Well, everyone else at the gym had one and was performing well. I wasn't doing well, so I know it's this that was the difference."*

In an intriguing manner that only Wil could pull off, he began to ask me questions that seemed so unrelated—to what we were speaking about before the package came, and to why I had the iPod sent to me.

Then he asked me to close my eyes while he prayed.

CHAPTER 4

As he prayed, he asked the Lord to show me things that have caused me hurt. There were many, actually, that went across my mind—whether manipulated by the "asking of God" that prompted it, I knew not. But then something unquestionable and undeniable happened.

I began to cry—silently at first, then to a level of uncontrollableness.

When I was able to respond to Will after he concluded his prayer, he asked me what caused the sobbing.

It was a time in my life at age 12-13, again, playing football. Besides my lack of real ability was the lack of equipment. Each one of the players were responsible to pay some equipment fees and provide their own cleats. That was not provided for me. It could've been, but was not a priority, so I went to practice without—each day.

Though I participated in all the drills and conditioning, when it came time to have live practice, I wasn't able to participate.

Except for a day that the coach felt sorry for me and asked another player to give me his pads so I could get a few plays in.

With pads not specific for me, and no cleats, it was a humiliating experience.

Sometime after that, a resolve was deposited in my soul—that I would never again go without what I need to be as adequate and seen as others. Nor would I let that happen to my children.

Wil Franz had spiritually and prayerfully led me into a deep flaw in my life that had affected me for 30 years!

Teaching in that session and the next day was centered around **episodic memory.**

A simple definition of episodic memory is the memory of autobiographical events (times, places, associated emotions, and other contextual who, what, when, where, why knowledge) that can be explicitly stated or conjured. (For example, a party when you were six years old).

Events that are recorded into episodic memory may trigger **episodic learning,** i.e., a change in behavior that occurs as a result of an event.

That is clearly what happened to me—lived out over three decades.

During the weekend, my Bible reading assignment included the life of Jacob. It was no accident. Maybe not intentional, but certainly sovereignly inspired by the Lord.

The chapters included Genesis 35, and these words struck me and caused the same emotion I had poured out on Thursday:

Genesis 35:1-3 (CSB)

God said to Jacob, "Get up! Go to Bethel and settle there. Build an altar there to the God who appeared to you when you fled from your brother Esau." So Jacob said to his family and all who were with him, "Get rid of the foreign gods that are among you. Purify yourselves and change your clothes. We must get up and go to Bethel. I will build an altar there to the God who answered me in my day of distress. He has been with me everywhere I have gone."

Jacob was being called back to a place of vulnerability and brokenness—yet surrendered to the Lord. It was a place and season in his life in which he sought God in his fear and inadequacy.

He built an altar, sought God and worshiped Him.

He needed the Lord.

He didn't allow his life to be shaped by what he believed he was—or was not—but rather on the esteem given to him *by God*.

For so long, he had operated on fear, the sense of lack, and the malpractice against him by his brother and father-in-law. He was even allowed to live that way due to his mother's cover-up and deceptive practices.

The gig was up.

The Lord was calling him back to Himself—in full trust.

When Jacob realized what the Lord was giving him an opportunity to do, he called his family to devotion.

Put away those idols! Purify yourself! We are going to Bethel—the House of God—and there I will build an altar.

What I didn't realize in my life was the **idols** I was carrying around with me—everywhere I went!

The idol of self-preservation.

The idol of self-protection.

The idol of independence.

And so many more.

On the run for decades—hiding from my guilt and shame, dodging vulnerability and transparency with God—the *gig for me was up!*

And here is what spoke to me so profoundly:

"To the God who answered me in the day of my distress AND has been with me EVERYWHERE I have gone!" (Genesis 35:3)

I spent years feeling inadequate—not having enough, or not having what others had. I lived for so many years *reeling* from moments in my life that seemed to mark me, shame me, and cause me humiliation.

I attempted to compensate by actually living according to my man-made *idols*.

I even imposed that on my family—without them knowing it—just as Jacob did.

But God!

When He came to me—through a man I thought strange—and through the Holy Spirit, who is able to *find you where you are living (or hiding!)*...

We do not need to be self-reliant and use whatever survival skills we can.

That's what the Lord called Jacob out of!

I could hear the Lord call me to Him, reminding me that—even through all of that—**He has been with me EVERYWHERE I have been** in my life.

It was life changing.

There was a hand still holding me, even when I didn't believe it.

There are a few things that I learned that I believe will help you:

1. **You can morph into who you become, even against who God created you to be.** Thus, you lose identity and unfortunately ask yourself, *"Who am I?"* Or just declare, *"I don't know who I am."*

2. **That morphed-into identity will reveal a locked-up heart**—not willing to say, *"Come and see"*,—because you will read the crowd to see where it is safe for you to hide, so you won't be wounded anymore. My fear of rejection, and inability to deal logically and rationally with people because of anxiety and conflict, and unresolved emotion caused me to focus on myself—being embarrassed, overly sensitive, and suspicious of people.

After receiving this information about myself, and walking through this with honesty, I began a journey toward healing and discovering who I was—and how to live that out.

Truly asking the Lord to examine us will help us in our relationship with Him, and the perfecting of holiness in our Christian walk.

Psalm 139:23-24 (CSB)

"Search me, God, and know my heart; test me and know my concerns. See if there is any offensive way in me; lead me in the everlasting way."

To be able to please God, there is the need to stop being distracted by the audience of men and women.

Part of that is learning to ask,

"Lord, what do you see of me?"

I get it—we fear exposure!

Yet we long for it… so we can be accepted and changed.

It takes a lot of effort to maintain an image that is never intended for you!

Application

1. **The Lord is wooing us out of distress into a place of freedom.**

Job 36:16 (ESV)

"He also allured you out of distress into a broad place where there was no cramping, and what was set on your table was full of fatness."

Job was certainly in a dark place—and spent chapters in the printed Bible declaring how God had abandoned him and done him wrong in the expected scheme of life.

He didn't understand what God had done, or what God was doing.

Since there was no answer or response from God, Job determined it would've been better if God had struck his day of birth out of existence!

It was the words of Elihu that truly expressed what God was doing for Job at this time of his life—words that seems so consistent with the providence of God in all of our lives:

Job 36:16 (MSG)

"Oh, Job, don't you see how God's wooing you from the jaws of danger? How he's drawing you into wide-open places—inviting you to feast at a table laden with blessings?"

2. **Our true identity and radiant hope are always in Christ alone.**

Galatians 2:20 (NLT)

"My old self has been crucified with Christ. It is no longer I who live, but Christ lives in me. So I live in this earthly body by trusting in the Son of God, who loved me and gave himself for me."

As Christians, when we fail to embrace God-defined identity, we are subject to our identity being shaped by culture, experiences, and what has been said about us by others.

Christ-esteem contrasts with self-esteem by emphasizing a person's worth and identity in Christ—rather than in their own achievements, abilities, or self-perception.

It is rooted in the belief that true confidence and value come from recognizing oneself as a child of God, redeemed and loved by Jesus—rather than relying on worldly success or personal accomplishments.

3. **Understanding our own identity in Christ motivates obedience according to who we are.**

Colossians 3:12-14 (NLT)

"Since God chose you to be the holy people he loves, you must clothe yourselves with tenderhearted mercy, kindness, humility, gentleness, and patience. Make allowance for each other's faults, and forgive anyone who offends you. Remember, the Lord forgave you, so you must forgive others. Above all, clothe yourselves with love, which binds us all together in perfect harmony."

Listen, you can only love others as you love yourself.

When your identity is whacked, and you lose yourself in what you have morphed into, the ability to express Christian character is not lost totally—but is certainly distorted.

We have been made new—to be true in created character, imputed in us by the Holy Spirit.

4. **Grow up "into" your new true identity—being conformed to the image of Christ.**

Romans 8:29 (ESV)

"For those whom he foreknew he also predestined to be conformed to the image of his Son, in order that he might be the firstborn among many brothers."

5. **Live in the God-rhythm of Life**

Romans 12:1-2 (NLT)

"And so, dear brothers and sisters, I plead with you to give your bodies to God because of all he has done for you. Let them be a living and holy sacrifice—the kind he will find acceptable. This is truly the way to worship him. Don't copy the behavior and customs of this world, but let God transform you into a new person by changing the way you think. Then you will learn to know God's will for you, which is good and pleasing and perfect."

As this chapter closes, let me share with you words often spoke to me by Wil Franz.

"Tyrone, the designed way to live is in the God-rhythm of life."

Every time I heard those words I could hear the softness of his voice that made the dictate sound easy.

It is *not*.
We have flesh that fights,
a mind that wanders,
and an attitude that rebels.

Yet, if we give ourselves over to the God who saved us—to develop and shape our way of living—it is easy.

Dear ones, having a reality of God being with you—*holding your hand, even when you didn't believe it*—may take a crisis of faith and trust.

Maybe a crisis in identity.

However, when He makes it evident, a distressed place becomes a place of freedom.

Practical Application

Reflection Questions:

1. When have you felt inadequate or lacking compared to others? How did this shape your behavior?

2. What "idols" might you be using to compensate for feelings of inadequacy?

3. How has God been present in your life, even when you didn't recognize it?

4. What does it mean to live in the "God-rhythm of life" in your current season?

Scripture References for Further Study:

- Genesis 35:1-3
- Psalm 139:23-24
- Job 36:16
- Galatians 2:20
- Romans 12:1-2

5

KEEP WALKING
WHEN FAITH REQUIRES ANOTHER STEP

> *"I might be down but I'm not dead;*
> *There's better days still ahead*
> *Even after all I've seen;*
> *There's hope in front of me"*
> —Danny Gokey, *Hope In Front of Me*

Leading a great and growing church, along with mentoring and supporting a couple dozen pastors, and guiding the CTC mission initiatives, leaves me limited time to do anything outside of ministry.

Serving on the coaching staff of Yuma Catholic High School has been one of those enjoyable commitments. Learning how to golf is a frustrating—yet enjoyable—hobby.

For many years daily workouts at a local gym was a very protected time slot. Rarely would I answer a call or return a text. Emails were seen by notifi-

CHAPTER 5

cation, but none were a priority—*unless* it was from an elder of CTC on the day of an elders' meeting.

Well, one workout happened with a message that has left an imprint in my heart to this day.

That particular workout was not only interrupted,

but even came to a **screeching halt**—

by an email from one of my beloved and trusted elders.

Our monthly elders' meeting was planned and set for that evening. Because of the content, it would have been another difficult one—but I wasn't concerned about that.

As a pastor, you don't want "yes men" alone as those who are biblically empowered and church-appointed to be your elders. Besides being biblically qualified, they should be men you know will speak truth and seek the Word for godly decisions and actions—no matter the desire of the pastor.

I can say the elders of CTC then (and now) were men of that coveted characteristic. So even anticipating tough meetings, it was welcomed.

I would tease that at times I'd leave an elders meeting to go watch a movie in which everyone gets killed!

And though I joked about that often—

this one was truly the only one that I wanted that to be true.

The email the elder sent was giving his resignation as an elder of CTC. I was *stunned*. There was no explanation given. So in the reply I asked was this resignation from the church also. The reply said "Yes, that is best".

This occurred while I was enduring a long separation that ended in divorce. Immediately, I presumed it was because of me and my personal situation—for what seemed like the one hundred and fiftieth time (the number of people that left our church during those years).

Shortly after wallowing in despair, a message came by text stating the decision to resign from CTC had *nothing to do with me or the church*. Other than that, no explanation was given.

The elders' meeting that evening began with me informing the remaining elders of the communication from the elder who resigned. No one knew what caused the resignation—leaving us all short of guessing, at least at first.

After discussing such, we began the meeting officially. The fiscal shape of the church was revealed in the financial reports. There were details discussed regarding our current state and future perspective.

It wasn't good.

Being joined in the discussion by our treasurer and administrator, I gave an explanation of how we managed financially the last few months. One way was moving reserved money from the missions account to the general account.

For a reason not clearly understood, one elder determined that the action was wrong, lacked integrity, and proved dishonesty—on my part. To be clear, it was *not* a decision I made nor could have made—on my own. But there was no opportunity to fully explain how that decision came to fruition.

The protesting elder stood up, threw his church keys on the table, and—with an eerie glee—shouted that he quit, as if it was orchestrated and planned.

Again, for the second time that day, I was stunned.

As if that was not enough to make a man quit the pastorate, there was another elder who was intent on me releasing the leadership role—but didn't actually have the courage to say so.

It was through other trusted men that a report was given to me of his belief and intent. That evening, after two elders quit, this elder also decided to attack personally. The remaining elders did well to protect me and challenge him. However, soon after, that elder also resigned.

CHAPTER 5

Elders resigning in our church context is not a light matter. Hearing the words of each one resigning, my emotional level rose. I wish I could say it was emotions of relief—as if each one resigning was good for the church.

Frankly, it was fear—

fear of this having a domino effect.

Every day that followed, the concern that the proverbial *"other shoe would drop"* was filling my head-space. What went along with that was a weighty heart. Grief, loss, and sorrow were part of my daily lunch box.

"Who else will leave?" was a constant question renting head space. Which, of course, led to the worse question a pastor has to work through: "Will the people trust me"?

The words of St Peter ring loud and true for me:

"Love covers a multitude of faults." (1 Peter 4:8).

Therefore, I do not share why staff is dismissed nor what events that may have caused elders to resign or be asked to step down. This is not to say that everyone this applies to has "faults' or is entirely at fault. However, whatever caused actions of the nature described above, I wouldn't share it. That left me vulnerable—which also caused me to lead with timidity and reservation.

From days to years that followed, church was as usual. *But I was not doing well.* We were not growing. Yet, there was a passion in me to faithfully carry out my calling.

A church in a larger city a few hours from Yuma that I was part of planting was in trouble. Though CTC was not in a solid position, we were stable. My passion, integrity to the call, and desire to help other pastors and churches inspired me to take on that problem and eventually make that church a campus of CTC. A church in that metro area saw what we did for the one church and asked if we would do the same for them.

To this day, I honestly cannot tell you whether it was the Lord, or me. I cannot say with confidence whether we should have done that or not. What I can say is it seemed the more I invested into the ministry and into pastoring, things that seemed to be stable became stagnant—and then it seemed they started to slowly die. By late spring of 2015, I knew I needed help—for me, and for the good of CTC.

Dave Patterson is the lead pastor of The Father's House in Vacaville, CA. TFH is a multi-campus church that serves as a hub to the nation for leadership, worship, and—above all—how to steward the Presence of God in all aspects of the church. The church he leads is renowned, and his leadership skills are noted nationally. I met Dave while we both were part of Minister's Fellowship International (MFI). His preaching was some of the best and most applicable to my ministry each time I had the opportunity to hear him. He also served briefly as a regional director for me in MFI. What I now know was inspired by the Spirit, I called Pastor Dave to let him know I needed help, and would he consider mentoring me.

There are three things with this call that I would say were wrought by the providence of God:

1. I hadn't spoken to Pastor Dave in several years. Yet, the Spirit prompted me to call him.
2. Dave answered on his off day—of all days.
3. He initiated a conversation and extended an invitation to TFH for observation.

In August of 2015, I spent three days with Pastor Dave and his Strategic Leadership Team. What was imparted in me is what was needed to take the passion and desire within me to pour into CTC for new life, growth, and impact in our city. It was incredible and has continued now for a decade. But that wasn't the most personally impactful event.

The first day at TFH, I returned from lunch to the church office for more meetings. When I walked into the reception area, the receptionist whose name

CHAPTER 5

is Shawna, whom I didn't know nor had met, asked if she could share with me what the Lord showed her about me. Without hesitation, I said, "Of course." What Shawna shared with such confidence and clarity, I had no doubt it was from the Lord.

I was walking through this field that had color, but it was dull. As I walked, however, the field not only lost color, but everything began to die. The dull color soon was lost as I kept walking, from dull to gray to colorless. That was hard to hear, but as Shawna kept talking, it got worse. As I kept walking, everything began to die. Now bones are very present, on the surface of dried, parched ground. I noticed how dead everything was and got a stark reality: I was walking into a place of death and darkness.

Now overwhelmed with what I am experiencing, with no end in sight, I reached down, picked up a skull, held it up to God and said, "Is this it? Is this what You promised me? Is this the best it gets? If so, I will still serve you." I threw down the skull, and then heard the words, "Keep walking."

As I did, things began to get color, and then living things, and then more color, and more life. Finally, I came to a bright door. I knew I was to open that door. And when I did, behind it were multitudes of people of all ethnicities and statuses in life, along with life farther than my eye could see.

For me, there is certainly a familiarity of the Lord speaking through prophetic words, visions, and even dreams. Often God has spoken, and each time there is excitement, and inspired hope that is virtually visible.

When Shawna spoke, I followed her words with tears—as she described what I had walked through and what was, at that very moment, still unfolding—to the near sight a father would have seeing his much-anticipated child coming through in delivery! All of the vision spoke to me at a time I really needed to hear a word of hope.

With it, I was also reminded of how God works in our darkness, as He leads us to *His* light. Often when God seems absent in moments of hardship, He is actually exercising His sovereignty to deliver good gifts of grace to His children.

Dear one, many times receiving the grace and gifts of God is found in your steps. **Keep walking!** Those steps may be the distance of where He is and where He wants you to be.

We have all been through moments—and possibly seasons—when you are doing what you believe the Lord has commissioned and called you to do, and yet you are confused about what He is doing. *"Is this what You promised me?"*

But as you read through biblical narratives, you will see that hardship and despairing times do not mean that God is absent. Nor does it mean that He is distant, uninvolved, or doesn't care. Behind these dark and dry valley moments is a God who is actively working for the good of His children.

A great opportunity as a pastor to inspire hope and preach on how God keeps His promises is Advent. Many in my congregation have not been raised in the tradition of Advent emphasis—as I was not—so I consider it important still for them to know what it means and why it is celebrated in churches in your neighborhood and around the world.

Advent is the season of the year leading up to Christmas. *Advent* means "arrival," "coming," or "appearing." It's a season where we remember not only Jesus' birth but also anticipate His promised return.

The Advent season lasts for four Sundays, beginning the fourth Sunday before Christmas, or the nearest Sunday to November 30. Advent ends on Christmas Eve. Each week of Advent focuses on a different theme—hope, peace, joy, and love.

Think of Advent as a time of waiting and preparation—looking back to Bethlehem, and looking forward to the day He will come again.

This is a season of hope, a time of anticipation. Imagine for a moment the people of Israel over 2,000 years ago. They knew the ancient prophecies and were waiting with hope. Day by day, they lived in anticipation, faithfully waiting for God's promise to come true. And then, it happened: Jesus was born. The waiting ended as God fulfilled His promise, giving His only Son as our Savior. Christmas happened because God kept His word.

The people of Israel would have sung songs which represents the cry while waiting:

O come, O come, Emmanuel,
And ransom captive Israel,
That mourns in lonely exile here
Until the Son of God appears.
Rejoice! Rejoice! Emmanuel shall come to thee, O Israel.

While Israel would have sung the song in expectation of Christ's first coming, the church now sings the song and expects the second coming in the future. We know that Jesus came and fulfilled the promises of God, but now we're awaiting His return. Every Advent season, we are reminded that just as God was faithful to fulfill His promise the first time, He will fulfill it again.

Now, let's give our attention to a passage of scripture that speaks to the hope, the joy, the peace, and the power of the Spirit that we experience as we await His soon return:

Romans 15:13 (ESV)

"May the God of hope fill you with all joy and peace in believing, so that by the power of the Holy Spirit you may abound in hope."

This verse concludes the doctrinal and application of Paul's writing regarding the gospel of Jesus Christ. Each word declares the manner in which we should live, as we wait for the Lord's return.

The expression *"the God of hope"* means the God who inspires hope is also the one who is able to fill us with peace, joy, and the Holy Spirit. Paul links these vital elements of the Christian to God as the source of every good thing.

Recently, I saw a pharmaceutical advertisement that brought the reality of people's hopelessness—causing them to grab anything that seems to promise any kind of help, no matter the side effects. The commercial was for Ingrezza, with its long list of side effects—including, ironically, the very symptom it's meant to treat.

This mirrors our world's desperate search for hope in everything *but* God.

If you do not have God, you will not—and cannot—have hope! Therefore, there is no hope for them in this world.

But if you have Christ, you have all the hope you need!

Just give me Jesus! Edward Mots expressed it in one of our best-known hymns:

My hope is built on nothing less,
Than Jesus' blood and righteousness;
I dare not trust the sweetest frame,
But wholly lean on Jesus' name.
On Christ, the solid Rock, I stand;
All other ground is sinking sand.

Practical Application

Reflection Questions:

1. When have you heard God say "keep walking" in your darkest valley?

2. How has God turned your "dull colors" into vibrant life?

3. What promises of God are you waiting to see fulfilled?

4. Where do you need to trust God's sovereignty in your current season?

Scripture References for Further Study:

- Romans 15:13
- Isaiah 40:31
- Psalm 130:5
- Hebrews 6:19
- 1 Peter 1:3

6

THERE IS AN ENEMY
STANDING FIRM WHEN DARKNESS PUSHES BACK

> *"No matter where I go, I won't be afraid, 'cause I know that I am not alone"*
> —Danny Gokey, *Hope In Front of Me*

> *"The thief comes only to steal and kill and destroy. I came that they may have life and have it more abundantly."*
> —John 10:10 (ESV)

For 21 years, I've been part of a coaching staff led by Rhett Stallworth. Three of those years were at our alma mater, Yuma High School, in Yuma, Arizona. Eighteen years of that were at Yuma Catholic High School.

Rhett is worthy of mention simply for his success. In 19 years as a head coach, he compiled a record of 190-48—an .850 winning percentage! From my research, it is the highest winning percentage in the state of Arizona. Besides winning three state championships in Arizona, he led teams to eight state championship games.

CHAPTER 6

However, Rhett is noteworthy not just for victories but for the lessons he taught young men, fellow coaches, and how he lived these principles out in real game situations. One particular game stands out as a clear demonstration of what spiritual warfare looks like when the enemy tempts you to accept defeat.

Down ten points to a team that would later become state champions at a higher division, Coach Stallworth orchestrated a plan with less than three minutes left in the game. During a crucial drive to get into the end zone, our quarterback, Stetson Stallworth (Coach's nephew), got flustered on a play, lost his composure, and was tackled for a loss at a critical moment.

The clock was ticking, our quarterback was shaken, and you could see hope draining from the players and coaches on the sidelines. Defeat seemed certain. But this time something was different.

This is a good place for me to share more about why this moment gets attention as being different. I've known Rhett Stallworth since he was about six years old. His older brother Steve (Stetson's father) and I were schoolmates and friends at Yuma High School, representing the Criminals tradition well. Along with sisters Brenda (who also was a schoolmate), Robyn, and Lori, and brother, Blake—they are just as much my family as *they* are family.

My relationship as friend, family, and pastor includes being the pastor of their late father, Richard. Knowing the patriarch brings clarity to the family dynamics. An intense, competitive, do-or-die grit was preached, practiced and expected. Each of the Stallworth siblings have that trait, in their own way. And in the success of each that I have witnessed in their life, you see that trait in one manner or another.

In Coach Rhett Stallworth, it is augmented. Though his heart expresses itself in a multitude of ways that certainly proves his Christian faith, Coach Stallworth is competitive, intense, and expects nothing less than perfect execution—especially when you are under pressure.

Stetson was his nephew, but that did not lessen what was expected next when he got shook, stumbled, and landed out of bounds for a loss at a crucial time. I didn't need to look in the stands behind me to see how the family was bracing themselves. Nor did I need to attempt to hear the sound from the crowd. Because there was none.

The players on the sideline were poised for a "descriptive" moment. A crowd of thousands was silent—braced and ready for what was next… or so we thought.

Normally, Coach Stallworth would come down hard for such a crucial mistake this late in the game. But this time, Coach got everyone's attention with what he said to Stetson, speaking calmly, yet with tremendous confidence:

"Relax, we got this."

The next play Coach called was "Boise"—a play we had practiced but wasn't in the plan for this game. It worked brilliantly, gaining 50 yards and positioning us less than five yards from the end zone. But time was ticking, and we were still down by two scores.

The next play Coach called was "Clemson"—another play we had practiced for four years but never used in a game! When the ball was snapped, our running back received it instead of the quarterback. The back ran outside, then handed it to a receiver on a reverse. As the receiver rounded the corner with defenders closing in, he threw the ball to our wide-open quarterback in the back of the end zone.

After the extra point, we were down by just three points—but only 1:34 remained on the clock.

Coach called for an onside kick, hoping one of our players would recover a bobble. It didn't happen. River Valley recovered the kickoff with just one task: run two plays to run out the clock. Hope dimmed again.

But then, remarkably, River Valley fumbled on their first play, and a Yuma Catholic defenseman recovered the ball!

What had been dashed hopes moments before transformed into renewed determination. With 1:15 left, we had possession at the 50-yard line. After three positive plays, our quarterback ran "Lucky Dog" into the end zone for a touchdown as the final seconds expired!

From the agony of defeat to the thrill of victory—"Lucky Dog" was the blessed hope for a coach who understood there is an enemy, but that enemy is not greater than the power of hope!

The world around us consists of much more than we can see. "Lucky Dog" was a success for Yuma Catholic Shamrocks that day, in that game.

The Bible clearly teaches that we live in a world with two realms: the natural and the spiritual. Our playbook does not have "Lucky Dog" as an option.

Living in these two realms the spiritual battles are daily. Or should I say—*hourly!* It is our position that gives us the advantage in this battle. As Christians, we sit and live in heavenly places at all times.

Ephesians 2:4-6 (NLT)

"But God is so rich in mercy, and he loved us so much, that even though we were dead because of our sins, he gave us life when he raised Christ from the dead. (It is only by God's grace that you have been saved!) For he raised us from the dead along with Christ and seated us with him in the heavenly realms because we are united with Christ Jesus."

"Seated" means "sitting with"—where life is happening. All our spiritual life flows from heaven and exists in heaven. We live in a heavenly realm. Our redemption, liberation, prayer life, worship, and communication with God happen because we live in this heavenly realm.

Yet, we still live here on earth in the natural realm. This is how Paul can describe each Christian as simultaneously seated with Christ "in heavenly places" while going about our everyday lives on earth (Eph. 3:10).

Though we sit in heavenly places, we, along with all humanity, live in a spirit world. Because our daily lives are physical in nature, it's easy to forget that the spiritual realm surrounds us. Though invisible, it's no less real than the world of our five senses. These two realms—the natural and spiritual—are distinct, yet clearly interact, creating constant spiritual conflict.

Assessing Our Enemy

Why is this conflict happening? Once a heavenly angel known as Lucifer rebelled against God's rule to establish his own. In Genesis, we see how through the serpent, he deceived Adam and Eve and usurped their God-given domain over the planet. That surrender placed Adam and Eve—and all of us—into a domain of darkness, the realm of the flesh and earthly living.

When Adam and Eve sinned, they surrendered their spiritual authority to the devil. Now we live daily life in Satan's domain—the kingdom of darkness. The Scriptures teach that the whole world is under Satan's influence—a powerful, supernatural being who is an absolute enemy of God, His creation, and His people.

1 John 5:19 (NIV)

> *"We know that we are children of God and that the world is under the control of the evil one."*

Satan's primary strategy has been to convince the world he doesn't exist. The Scriptures clearly acknowledge his existence and influence.

In his insightful book *The Screwtape Letters,* C.S. Lewis writes: "There are two equal and opposite errors into which our race can fall about the devils. One is to disbelieve in their existence, and the other is to believe, and to feel an excessive and unhealthy interest in them."[9]

While we need not become consumed with the demonic—neither fascinated by nor anxious about their activities—we do need to know enough about our enemy to be effective in the fight. The modern Western world may scoff at spiritual warfare, but this plays directly into the hands of a thief and murderer who can do his work unnoticed and unseen. The devil wants nothing less than our destruction and complete ineffectiveness as witnesses of Christ.

Another of Satan's strategies I've witnessed having a crippling effect on believers is **shattering their hope.** The devil can put up such an aggressive front that defeat or failure seems inevitable. Instead of fighting through and against him, many give up.

> "Satan's primary strategy has been to convince the world he doesn't exist."

I've seen the anointed man of God clearly called to plant a church who abandoned hope when his wife was diagnosed with cancer. I've known the passionate woman excited about her nonprofit partnership to support widows who gave up her dream to care for her ailing mother. And I've witnessed the young man preparing for youth ministry who walked away when faced with a false accusation.

Each of these represents real obstacles—that's part of life. Challenges occur. Speed bumps may slow us down. However, the enemy magnifies these obstacles, penetrating your heart, mind, and emotions until you accept defeat.

The spiritual warfare lessons from that football game are glaring:

First, there was a calming, assuring effect from the coach to the quarterback that resembles the confident assurance we hear from the Lord during our personal battles:

1 John 4:4 (CSB)

"You are from God, little children, and you have conquered them, because the one who is in you is greater than the one who is in the world."

Second is the preparation for readiness. The team had practiced plays we didn't know when we would use, yet that preparation proved critical. The strength was in the readiness. The security came from knowing that the one in charge—our Coach—was sure in what he had done to prepare us, in spite of the enemy's movements.

Isn't that what we can rest in with our God?

Psalm 18:32 (NIV)

"It is God who arms me with strength and keeps my way secure."

Finally, knowing your enemy is crucial. Coach Stallworth meticulously broke down the traits and characteristics of every team we played. There wasn't any regular player on opposing teams whose tendencies weren't known to us.

Similarly, **2 Corinthians 2:11** reminds us not to be ignorant of Satan's devices, so he doesn't take advantage of us!

What made "Boise," "Clemson," and "Lucky Dog" so effective was that no one had seen us run them before. Though practiced for years, they remained unused until the critical moment. When the game was on the line, knowing the enemy's strategy and having prepared to follow our leader made the difference between defeat and victory. The spiritual warfare lessons are clear!

We do ourselves a disservice by not recognizing that standing for Jesus and His kingdom brings us into conflict with God's staunch enemy. Satan's attacks mean we're all vulnerable to sickness, betrayal, financial meltdown, relational loss, emotional despair, and other hardships.

One primary solution Scripture gives to the problem of why bad things happen to good people is that we live in a war zone.

Participation in this war isn't optional but an unavoidable reality of the Christian life. Just like a war in the natural realm, we ignore the enemy at our peril. We're not at war with people but with the enemy and the dark powers of this present age who influence our world. This is truly spiritual warfare and must be fought using divinely powerful weapons.

Paul held this warfare worldview and warned us that the devil schemes against us:

Ephesians 6:12 (NIV)

"For our struggle is not against flesh and blood, but against the rulers, against the authorities, against the powers of this dark world and against the spiritual forces of evil in the heavenly realms."

We have an active role in standing against the enemy's schemes. Peter warns us to be serious and alert because the enemy is like a lion on the hunt. If we're nonchalant in our approach to spiritual warfare, we can incur real harm. We're commanded to actively resist the devil. In war, there will be times of active fighting and lulls in between, but our default position should be alertness and sobriety.

1 Peter 5:8-9 (ESV)

"Be sober-minded; be watchful. Your adversary the devil prowls around like a roaring lion, seeking someone to devour. Resist him, firm in your faith..."

There's a popular notion that becoming a follower of Jesus leads to an easier life, when actually troubles and persecutions often come as a result.

As Charles Spurgeon once said, "Satan never kicks a dead horse." Christians who take their faith seriously are targets of the devil. It's the Church, after all, that's tearing down his strongholds, demolishing his kingdom, and releasing his captives.

In this way, we can be encouraged by opposition, for it shows we're on the right track! But we need not fear. The Spirit of God is leading us in this fight.

2 Corinthians 10:3-4 (ESV)

"For though we walk in the flesh, we are not waging war according to the flesh. For the weapons of our warfare are not of the flesh but have divine power to destroy strongholds."

Satan and the demonic are created beings and no match for God. They aren't omnipresent or omnipotent. They're limited in power and influence, but their power still has real consequences. We should never fear the enemy, but we should respect what he's capable of.

Christ Has Overcome

God and Satan aren't on equal footing. It's Creator versus created. Though Satan has power, it's nothing compared to the omnipotence of God. With a word, He could wipe out Satan and his army—and in Revelation 19, at the end of time, we see exactly this as Christ conquers all demonic powers.

He wins. Every. Single. Time.

God rules over history, and His purposes will be accomplished. We can rest in this truth. We have nothing to fear. The decisive and final victory over evil and the evil one was accomplished on the cross. Jesus, by His death and resurrection, took away the power of the evil one, who no longer has dominion over those who are in Christ.

1 John 3:8b (NIV)

"The reason the Son of God appeared was to destroy the works of the devil."

It's of primary importance we understand that God was, is, and will be the winner of this battle. The New Testament clearly states that the life, death, and resurrection of Jesus signaled a decisive victory by God over the kingdom of darkness. As Paul explains:

Colossians 2:15 (ESV)

"[God] disarmed the rulers and authorities and put them to open shame, by triumphing over them in him."

By His death on the cross, Christ paid the debt for our sin, disarming His enemies and putting them to shame. Satan and his angels lost the battle once and for all. Jesus will soon return to deliver *"the kingdom to God the Father after destroying every rule and every authority and power"* (1 Cor. 15:24).

Romans 16:20 (CSB)

"The God of peace will soon crush Satan under your feet. The grace of our Lord Jesus be with you."

Practical Application

God has equipped us with offensive weapons:

Ephesians 6:13-18 (CSB)

"For this reason take up the full armor of God, so that you may be able to resist in the evil day, and having prepared everything, to take your stand. Stand, therefore, with truth like a belt around your waist, righteousness like armor on your chest, and your feet sandaled with readiness for the gospel of peace. In every situation take up the shield of faith with which you can extinguish all the flaming arrows of the evil one. Take the helmet of salvation and the sword of the Spirit—which is the word of God."

This spiritual armor prepares us to face any spiritual battle. These battles aren't fought against *"flesh and blood"* enemies but against the *"powers of this dark world."* We cannot defeat Satan in our own strength, and we can't fight spiritual battles without God's protection and weapons. God provides supernatural defense by giving us His Holy Spirit and His armor.

There are six elements of God's armor. Each one is as important as the others, and we can't be fully armed without putting on all pieces:

1. **THE BELT OF TRUTH:** All truth is God's truth. As followers of Jesus, we should pursue all truth.

    Satan is the master deceiver who twists truth and adds lies that seem right. The more we embrace truth, the better we can detect Satan's destructive spin. As Christ followers, it is the belt of truth that assures us of being right when the world, and the media challenges what we believe.

The foundation of spiritual, moral, and relational truth comes from the Bible. Jesus promises,

John 8:31–31

"If you hold to my teaching, you are really my disciples. Then you will know the truth, and the truth will set you free."

2. **THE BREASTPLATE OF RIGHTEOUSNESS:** Righteousness is imputed to us based on Christ's sacrifice. Though we aren't righteous, we're made righteous in Christ Jesus. What you have become regulates your behavior. When we are righteous, we don't give Satan a foothold that he can use to tear us down.

   Most importantly, this righteousness isn't ours—it's Christ's. We're righteous only because of Christ within us. Therefore, the breastplate of righteousness is the protector of what has been given us when we confessed Christ as our Lord and Savior.

3. **FEET FITTED WITH READINESS FROM THE GOSPEL OF PEACE:** The foundation of our armor is our footwear. We stand on the gospel—the foundational truth that God created you, Jesus saved you from sin, and the Holy Spirit is restoring you and the world.

   Satan brings strife, confusion, and division. The gospel brings peace. Wherever your feet go, peace follows. It is the sandals of the gospel of peace that allows us to walk through situations of chaos in our lives, bringing peace and an opportunity for others to have this peace also.

4. **THE SHIELD OF FAITH:** Unbelief and doubt are the enemy's temptations during suffering, accusations, and difficulties. Faith protects us from fiery darts so we can stay fixed on God's promises.

   Hoisting up the shield of faith in the face of a doctor's fatal report, or news of your job being terminated, or even a relationship you invested in threatening to sabotage your life will be the piece of armor that sustains you.

5. **THE HELMET OF SALVATION:** Salvation isn't just what happened when we trusted Jesus—it also means the eventual reality that our victory as followers of Jesus is assured. Satan wants us to believe that sin and bad habits define us. Be convinced of what Christ has done and reject any thoughts contrary to the knowledge of God. Put on that helmet when the accuser of the brethren provokes and makes his case against you! Your mind will become full of the words of Christ: *You are justified and glorified in Him.*

6. **THE SWORD OF THE SPIRIT:** The only *offensive* weapon in the armor is the Sword of the Spirit—the Word of God. Jesus used it to put the devil to flight. It strikes a blow to the enemy even today.

   Of course, it's only as we read, study, memorize, and practice God's Word that it becomes alive and active in our lives. The Sword of the Spirit is to be a lifetime companion in your life—not just attached to your side, but put in practice, daily. You cannot live by bread alone, but every word that proceeds from the mouth of God.

You can do this! There is an enemy with a plan for your life—but it's for destruction. Christ came to destroy the enemy's works and give you life in abundance. Since He has freed you, it's on you to walk in that freedom. Jesus has set us free! Therefore: *be strong in the Lord and in the strength of His might (Ephesians 6:10)* and live in confidence!

1 John 5:4-5 (NLT)

"For every child of God defeats this evil world, and we achieve this victory through our faith. And who can win this battle against the world? Only those who believe that Jesus is the Son of God."

Reflection Questions:

1. When have you felt the enemy's attack most strongly in your life? How did God's presence and power help you through that time?

2. Which piece of the armor of God do you most need to strengthen in your life right now? What practical steps can you take to do so?

3. How might recognizing we're in a spiritual battle change the way you respond to difficulties and challenges?

4. In what ways have you seen God turn what seemed like certain defeat into victory in your own life?

Scripture References for Further Study:

- 2 Corinthians 2:11
- James 4:7
- Revelation 12:10-11
- Luke 10:19
- 2 Timothy 1:7
- 1 John 4:4
- Romans 8:37-39

7

FAITH IS NOT A FIX
FINDING GOD'S LOVE IN SEASONS OF SUFFERING

> *"There's a story that I should have died, but these broken parts are stronger now"*
> —Danny Gokey, *Hope In Front of Me*

Job 19:25–27 (CSB)

> *"But I know that my Redeemer lives, and at the end he will stand on the dust. Even after my skin has been destroyed, yet I will see God in my flesh. I will see him myself; my eyes will look at him, and not as a stranger. My heart longs within me."*

I remember sitting in the quiet of my office, staring at the email that had just arrived. Another pastor—one I knew and respected—had taken his own life. This wasn't the first such message I'd received in recent years. The weight of it pressed on my chest like a stone.

How does someone who preaches hope every Sunday reach such a point of hopelessness?

CHAPTER 7

How does a person who regularly reminds others of God's faithfulness come to believe that God has abandoned them?

These questions led me back to a book of Scripture that has become, perhaps surprisingly, one of my favorites—**Job.**

While many find its pages difficult to read, I approach them with excitement and anticipation. Each January, as I begin my chronological reading of the Bible, I encounter Job's story concurrent with events in Genesis.

As difficult as it is to witness Job's suffering, the Lord reveals His love and faithfulness through it all, proving Himself good in the end.

The Bible doesn't tell us exactly how long Job suffered. We know his suffering began with the death of his servants and the loss of his livestock, progressing to the deaths of his children and his own physical afflictions. Scripture suggests these calamities occurred in a single day, with messengers arriving one after another while *"the previous one was yet speaking"* (Job 1:16-18).

Job's three friends—Eliphaz, Bildad, and Zophar—came when they heard of his suffering (Job 2:11). What we don't know is how long after Job's suffering began did they hear the news, or how long it took them to travel to him. When they arrived, they sat in silence with him for seven days.

We're not told over how many days their subsequent conversations took place, or how long Elihu spoke after them, or even how long God's discourse with Job lasted.

Following this chronology without definitive time markers, we can't know precisely how long Job suffered. We can reason it must have been more than a few weeks based on the sequence of events: the day of calamity, the time for news to reach his friends, their journey to him, a week of silent mourning, extended conversations, God's intervention, and finally Job's restoration.

Some scholars suggest these events may have transpired over two years, while others propose 42 months, echoing the Great Tribulation. But there's no way to determine the exact duration of Job's suffering.

When God allows suffering in our lives—whether for days, months, or years—we must remember He has a purpose. We're promised He works all things for our good and His glory. What matters most isn't the length or severity of our suffering but how we suffer. Where do we turn for comfort and hope?

It's my belief that Job's deepest anguish stemmed from his feeling that God had abandoned him. Job admitted, *"I have uttered what I did not understand"* (Job 42:5). His understanding was based on the belief that earthly blessings were gifts from God and that God protected the faithful from harm. When Job's possessions and children were taken, he may have concluded God had abandoned him. Yet, remarkably, *"he did not sin by charging God with wrongdoing"* (Job 1:22).

I believe Job's greatest suffering was thinking God had turned away from him. Reading his words in that light, we see a man despairing, feeling alone, and grieving his perceived distance from God.

Job never learned why such calamities befell him. God never explained it. But eventually, God revealed more of Himself to Job, giving him comfort and hope. And then, God restored what Job had lost, blessing him doubly.

The greatest restoration in Job's story wasn't his wealth or children but his experience of God's presence. The book begins with Job offering sacrifices for his children (Job 1:5) and ends with God telling Job's friends to offer sin sacrifices while instructing Job to pray for them.

When Job obeyed, he demonstrated his continuing faith that God was present to hear his prayers. Rather than judging Job, God commended him (Job 42:7-8), restored him (Job 42:9-10), and gave him a long, full life (Job 42:17).

Bob Clark was a supporter of me as a pastor, and of Church For The City in the early days of 1993. His family was a model Christian family. Jackie is a Proverbs 31 woman—in real life! Their sons, Joel, Micah, and Stephen loved their parents, the church, and enjoyed life.

CHAPTER 7

Bob was a very successful insurance man for many years in Yuma. As a churchman, he served passionately. Bob supported the ministry, encouraged me in my preaching, and honored more than I deserved. His love for me and my family was evident in his prayers and generosity.

The parent company of Bob's insurance agency did not approve some sales that were part of Bob's business. Instead of working toward a resolution, they unjustly pulled the clients from Bob's agency. All that he worked for—which he used generously, and lived a comfortable lifestyle—was taken by one action; unprecedented and not foreseen.

Because Bob could not find work in Yuma that was equal to his ability and income, his family sold their home here and moved closer to Jackie's family in Idaho.

Before Bob left Yuma he fell off his roof, as they were preparing and packing to leave. His final call to me while in Yuma, before his departure, included words similar to this:

"Pastor, I am on my way out of Yuma. The Lord has blessed me here and I believe I have been a blessing to many here. But the trials of Job, from the Lord, have struck me. My trust in God will remain, yet, I am experiencing an injustice, as did Job".

The Clark family settled in the Boise area, and the family has done well. The family has been successful—vocationally and spiritually. Bob preaches a strong word of the Lord, serves in missions (including going with me to Northern India), ministers prophetically, and is still a great blessing and encouragement to me.

The Lord does restore, as we place our hope and trust in Him.

Understanding how God worked sovereignly in Job's life—commending, restoring, and rewarding him—has deepened my compassion for those who feel driven to suicide, including, sadly, many pastors. Recent research reveals that loneliness plays a significant role in this crisis. Each time I hear of another pastor's death—which feels intensely personal when I learn it from someone close to the deceased—I ask, "How do we make sense of this?"

We live in a culture that has experienced quantum leaps in medical science and technology, increasing average lifespans. Unfortunately, this can mean those who are elderly, terminally ill, or disabled may endure longer periods of suffering and loneliness. The fragility of our health occupies our thoughts.

Christians aren't immune to these concerns. Many of us hold theological positions suggesting that sickness, disease, and death are things God intends to heal and banish, proving His power and our faith. Yet too often, we fail to connect the fall of man into sin with our physical and mental health challenges.

The realities we face daily are starker than we care to admit. A young corporate rising star full of promise can die in a hit-and-run while jogging before work. A mother who sacrificed her Ivy League career to raise her children in godliness can receive a terminal cancer diagnosis before her youngest can even feed himself. A God-fearing, community-minded church man can wake to find his wife gone because she's chosen another relationship.

And we've seen pastors—not hypocrites like Saul or the guilt-ridden like Judas, but those bearing fruit, holding sound theology, never shirking challenges—take their own lives. This is suffering on an incalculable scale. As has been said, "Suicide is the ultimate act of despair."

Like Job, many of these individuals were deeply devoted to God. Job was happy, wealthy, wise, and his family not only knew their father's piety but trusted in his daily devotion to cover their imperfections. Yet God allowed Satan to test Job. This is theologically challenging but undeniable: God foreknew and sanctioned Job's testing (Job 1:6-12). What followed were the ill-advised words of friends expressing their opinions about Job's situation.

We don't have insight into God's inner thoughts or purposes. Nor does He typically tell us directly why difficulties occur in our lives. Since that's true, we draw our own conclusions.

CHAPTER 7

For many of us, the question becomes: Why is God hiding His face from me? For Job, however, he wanted to know when God would forgive him, look away, and leave him alone (Job 7:15, 19-21).

Times of suffering like Job's cause many to turn away from God. You've heard it—maybe even said it yourself: *"If God were good and all-powerful, He could stop my suffering!"* When He doesn't, we try to rationalize His purpose. I've concluded that my lack of answers doesn't mean answers don't exist.

So Much for Common Sense

The Psalmist Asaph was troubled when common sense didn't apply to his life:

Psalm 73:1-14 (NLT)

"Truly God is good to Israel, to those whose hearts are pure. But as for me, I almost lost my footing. My feet were slipping, and I was almost gone. For I envied the proud when I saw them prosper despite their wickedness. They seem to live such painless lives; their bodies are so healthy and strong. They don't have troubles like other people; they're not plagued with problems like everyone else. They wear pride like a jeweled necklace and clothe themselves with cruelty. These fat cats have everything their hearts could ever wish for! They scoff and speak only evil; in their pride they seek to crush others. They boast against the very heavens, and their words strut throughout the earth. And so the people are dismayed and confused, drinking in all their words. "What does God know?" they ask. "Does the Most High even know what's happening?" Look at these wicked people—enjoying a life of ease while their riches multiply. Did I keep my heart pure for nothing? Did I keep myself innocent for no reason? I get nothing but trouble all day long; every morning brings me pain."

Asaph knew that God was good to Israel—covenant Israel. He also perceived that God was good to people with pure hearts—like himself! Yet he struggled to understand how God allowed those outside the covenant family to prosper while he suffered. He went so far as to say he had remained clean and innocent in vain (vs. 13-14).

God answers this lack of common sense with God-sense! All is answered by God's own wisdom:

Psalm 73:15-26 (NLT)

"If I had really spoken this way to others, I would have been a traitor to your people. So I tried to understand why the wicked prosper. But what a difficult task it is! Then I went into your sanctuary, O God, and I finally understood the destiny of the wicked. Truly, you put them on a slippery path and send them sliding over the cliff to destruction. In an instant they are destroyed, completely swept away by terrors. When you arise, O Lord, you will laugh at their silly ideas as a person laughs at dreams in the morning. Then I realized that my heart was bitter, and I was all torn up inside. I was so foolish and ignorant—I must have seemed like a senseless animal to you. Yet I still belong to you; you hold my right hand. You guide me with your counsel, leading me to a glorious destiny. Whom have I in heaven but you? I desire you more than anything on earth. My health may fail, and my spirit may grow weak, but God remains the strength of my heart; he is mine forever."

When we step out from under the dark, mysterious shadow of God's ways and enter the place of His awe-inspiring presence—the sanctuary—we recognize that God will ultimately act justly. Whatever is happening in the present isn't the whole or final story.

Our Faith is Not a Fix

Bad things happen to bad people. Good things happen to bad people. But it's not correct to say bad things happen to good people because *"there is none good, no, not one"* (Romans 3:23).

God's hand of Providence is often hidden from us. When God smiles on us (Numbers 6:26) or is grieved with our actions, that doesn't indicate His ultimate path for us. We can't fully sort it out. So we must let God be God!

Satan still seeks to seduce us into believing we can't completely trust God. His deception is that God is either not good enough or powerful enough to address our suffering. Yet God does triumph for us, and Satan can do nothing about that.

> "Christianity isn't a tool of personal therapy. Yet Christianity is right, good, and alone in the promise of a faith that prevails."

Our God is our Redeemer who crushed the head of Satan as prophesied (Genesis 3:15) and affirmed (Romans 16:20). On the cross, He banished sin and the triumph of evil from our presence forever. Everything will be made right.

Christianity isn't true because it "works." Some actually admit that Christian faith alone doesn't work as a fix for what we want fixed. Christianity isn't a tool of personal therapy. Yet Christianity is right, good, and alone in the promise of a faith that prevails. God has overcome sin and death through Christ's cross and resurrection. The rumors of grace, forgiveness, and the redemption of all things are true.

Everything is going to be alright.

Love Poured In

Suffering in Greek is *thlipsis,* meaning affliction, distress; an oppressive state of physical, mental, social, or economic adversity; tribulation, trouble, persecution, pressure.

Suffering is experienced by Christ-followers and non-Christians alike. For every believer battling cancer, there's a non-believer facing the same diagnosis. For every Christian who loses a child, there's a non-Christian enduring the same loss.

The difference isn't in what happens but in our response and what it produces in us. People respond in various ways, but how should followers of Christ respond to suffering?

Negative responses are common among both Christians and non-Christians:

1. *Epicureanism,* from the Greek philosopher Epicurus (342-270 B.C.), taught that life is an inevitable mixture of good and bad experiences, so we should live life with more pleasure than pain to ensure a positive balance.

2. *Stoicism,* developed by Greek philosophers called Stoics, advised us to "grin and bear it."

Paul says Christians respond to trials by rejoicing in them, however strange or irrational this may seem to unbelievers. This response is evidence of salvation. And we can respond this way because of the love the Father pours into us!

Romans 5:3-5 (ESV)

"Not only that, but we rejoice in our sufferings, knowing that suffering produces endurance, and endurance produces character, and character produces hope, and hope does not put us to shame, because God's love has been poured into our hearts through the Holy Spirit who has been given to us."

The affliction, no matter how great, produces something in you of greater value than a pain-free life.

God's Purposes in Suffering

1. *Corrective suffering:* Suffering meant to return us to righteousness when we've strayed. If God brings this kind of suffering, we should confess and return to His path.

2. *Suffering for God's glory:* In John 9, Jesus healed a man blind from birth. When asked about the cause of his blindness, Jesus answered, *"Neither this man nor his parents sinned, but this happened so that the work of God might be displayed in his life"* (v. 3). This idea can be difficult to accept until we remember that life is short compared to eternity, and our chief purpose is to glorify God—by whatever means He chooses.

3. *Suffering as part of cosmic warfare:* Job was happy and favored, with a fine family and many possessions. Then suddenly he lost everything and didn't know why. But we know it was because of a conflict between Satan and God. God allowed Satan access to Job to show that Job loved God for Himself, not for blessings.

   Job lost everything, yet still worshipped God:

   "Naked I came from my mother's womb, and naked I will depart. The Lord gave and the Lord has taken away; may the name of the Lord be praised" (Job 1:21). This explanation accounts for much of what some Christians endure.

4. *Constructive suffering:* God uses our troubles, trials, and tribulations to form Christian character.

This doesn't mean we're glad or praise God thoughtlessly, but we rejoice in suffering (not for it) because we know its benefits. As Psalm 119:71 says: *"It was good that I was afflicted."*

What's Worked in Us

1. *Perseverance:* Also translated "patience," "endurance," or "patient endurance." The Greek word *hypomonē* means to "live under something." Combined with the word for tribulation, it means living under difficult circumstances without trying to escape them.

   As Proverbs 24:10 (NLT) says: *"If you fail under pressure, your strength is too small."*

2. *Character:* The Greek word *dokimē* is based on *dokimos,* meaning "tested" or "approved."

   As 1 Peter 1:7 (NLT) explains: *"These trials will show that your faith is genuine. It is being tested as fire tests and purifies gold—though your faith is far more precious than mere gold. So when your faith remains strong through many trials, it will bring you much praise and glory and honor on the day when Jesus Christ is revealed to the whole world."*

In suffering, God may prune bad habits, free you from idols, or simply allow you to experience His sufficiency. As Corrie ten Boom, who survived Nazi concentration camps, said: "I never really knew that God was all I needed until He was literally all I had."

These trials don't work against us but further our hope in God:

2 Corinthians 4:17 (NLT)

"For our present troubles are small and won't last very long. Yet they produce for us a glory that vastly outweighs them and will last forever!"

James 1:2-3 (NLT)

"Dear brothers and sisters, when troubles of any kind come your way, consider it an opportunity for great joy. For you know that when your faith is tested, your endurance has a chance to grow."

While I was in Junction City, Oregon during the fall of 1996 and winter of 1997, enrolled in the School of Restoration, the lessons I needed to learn were hard. Spiritually, I was more unaligned with the Lord and His Spirit than I had recognized. My marriage, then, was on the brink of destruction. My family was very vulnerable, for several reasons, including the fact that I was absent for almost seven months.

Along with that were relationships I was subject to in the community of where I lived. Many were very good, but some were challenging me personally.

One particular assignment was moving some plants from one spot in the landscape to another. It was not a significant move at all. As a matter of fact, it seemed senseless. We are talking a few feet that didn't change the look of the landscape at all.

I could not understand it, until there was an impression from the Spirit that caused me to reflect on James 1:2-3. It wasn't an assignment to move the plants. It was a God-directed opportunity for me to endure the inner trial of questioning, not understanding, and giving room to rebellion.

My faith was being tested in what God knew was best for me to grow. Is it based on what I think I need and what I should do? Or is it truly an opportunity for me to consider the tests God allows—for me to be joyful at the growth He was orchestrating and working in my life?

James 1:12 (NLT)

"God blesses those who patiently endure testing and temptation. Afterward they will receive the crown of life that God has promised to those who love him."

3. *Hope:* Finally, Paul indicates that the steadfast, approved character created by perseverance produces hope. It's because sufferings lead to endurance, endurance to an approved character, and character to an even more steadfast hope. All this further evidences our security in Christ.

Hope Without Disappointment

Romans 5:5a (NLT)

"And this hope will not lead to disappointment."

Every other hope will disappoint! Whether in horoscopes, people, or perfect circumstances—all are "mights," but nothing is assured.

Paul says, "I have a better hope than any of these things! One that does not disappoint!" Hope that doesn't disappoint or make us ashamed isn't just in the future—but also in the present.

2 Timothy 1:12 (NLT)

> *"That is why I am suffering here in prison. But I am not ashamed of it, for I know the one in whom I trust, and I am sure that he is able to guard what I have entrusted to him until the day of his return."*

Though suffering as an apostle, Paul felt no shame. He knew in whom he believed and that God would guard him until the Day. His present conditions didn't shame him or diminish his hope for future glory. Look at Stephen (Acts 7) and martyrs throughout the ages. All died gloriously! The vision of glory they were certain of wasn't affected by their present suffering. Why?

God's Love Poured in Us by the Holy Spirit

Romans 5:5b (NLT)

> *"For we know how dearly God loves us, because he has given us the Holy Spirit to fill our hearts with his love."*

This is the first mention of the Holy Spirit in Romans, and He is the installment of God's love in our hearts.

Love here is *agape*—God's love toward us that comes only from Him. He doesn't love because of something or in spite of something. He doesn't love because He had no option or because we did something to deserve it. God's love is undeserved.

As a sinner ignorant of His goodness and desires for my life—disobedient, rebellious, carried away in selfishness—yet He pours His love into me like a flood!

> "You cannot have God's love poured into your heart and not know it! His love always leads to 'Hallelujah!'"

CHAPTER 7

Ephesians 2:4 (NLT)

"But God is so rich in mercy, and he loved us so much"

The Holy Spirit fills us with God's love, just as Jesus promised:

John 14:16-18 (NLT)

"I will ask the Father, and he will give you another Advocate, who will never leave you. He is the Holy Spirit, who leads into all truth. The world cannot receive him, because it isn't looking for him and doesn't recognize him. But you know him, because he lives with you now and later will be in you. No, I will not abandon you as orphans—I will come to you."

- Jesus knows life will include suffering for all of us.
- He knows we cannot endure it or maintain hope without help.
- The Holy Spirit is promised to relieve our feelings of abandonment and helplessness.
- Not everyone receives this help—doubters of God, rejecters, the indifferent, atheists, and agnostics will experience suffering too.
- The difference is that with the Spirit, suffering won't crush you or leave you hopeless; rather, you remain full of hope as you endure, build character, and become better.
- Why? Because God pours His comforting, assuring love into you—the love that says "you will make it, I've got you."
- It's poured out like water from above—a waterfall, a hurricane of love!
- Into every part of us: heart, the very center of our being.

You cannot have God's love poured into your heart and not know it! His love always leads to "Hallelujah!"

Unfortunately it is often the opposite that takes place with us. If pain is there, then we equate that to God *isn't*. If we are not feeling an overlay of the pain, then there is no comfort. What I've come to learn is that it's quite the contrary to the way of God.

When speaking of God's presence during suffering, Dr. Martyn Lloyd-Jones shared a letter written by Henry Venn, a Church of England vicar who died in 1797. He wrote this letter after his wife's death left him with five children to raise alone—a tragedy that could leave anyone feeling hopeless, abandoned, and in darkness. Henry Venn wrote to the Countess of Huntingdon:

"I am now a living witness of the truth you so strenuously maintain, and of necessity of that truth in our miserable condition here below. Did I not know the Lord to be mine, were I not certain his heart feels even more love for me than I am able to conceive, were not this evident to me, not by deduction and argument, but by consciousness, by His own light shining in my soul as the sun does upon my bodily eyes, into what a deplorable situation should I have been now cast?

"I have lost all that I could wish myself to have been, in the partner of my cares and joys, and lost her when her industry and ingenuity and tender love and care for her children were all just beginning to be perceived by the two eldest girls, and to strike them with a sense of the excellency of such qualities. I have lost her when her soul was as a watered garden, when her mouth was opened to speak for God, and He was blessing the testimony she bore to a free, full and everlasting pardon in the blood of Jesus. Nevertheless I can say, it is well; Hallelujah! For the Lord God Omnipotent reigns.

"At all times and in everything pertaining to me, let Him do what seems Him good. Then, and yet more important: 'were there no Holy Ghost now to strengthen me mightily, were there nothing more than a dependence of the word of promise, without an Almighty power and agent to explain, impress and apply it, how would my hands hang down, and my knees be so feeble that I should faint and fall under the pressure of my cross'. But on the

> "Faith is not the fix without The Man of Sorrows who knows suffering and pours His love into us as we suffer."

contrary, I abound in hope through the power of the Holy Ghost given unto me. I rejoice in tribulation, from the experience I now have, more than I possibly could in less a severe trial. The Man of Sorrows is as rivers of water in a dry place, and gives songs in the night."[10]

Well, there it is! Faith is not the fix without The Man of Sorrows who knows suffering and pours His love into us as we suffer. It is that love that assures us of His presence and expands our understanding of the depths of His love. Suffering comes. It can lead us into dark places with no hope. But love comes down and fills us with the fullness of God.

Ephesians 3:16-19 (CSB)

"I pray that he may grant you, according to the riches of his glory, to be strengthened with power in your inner being through his Spirit, and that Christ may dwell in your hearts through faith. I pray that you, being rooted and firmly established in love, may be able to comprehend with all the saints what is the length and width, height and depth of God's love, and to know Christ's love that surpasses knowledge, so that you may be filled with all the fullness of God."

Practical Application

For those experiencing suffering in their lives:

1. **Acknowledge the pain.** God doesn't ask us to pretend everything is fine. The Psalms are filled with honest expressions of grief, confusion, and pain. Like Job, we can bring our raw emotions before God.

2. **Seek God's presence, not just answers.** Job never received an explanation for his suffering, but he did receive God Himself. In your darkest moments, pursue God's presence rather than just understanding.

3. **Allow the Holy Spirit to comfort you.** The Spirit has been given as our Comforter. Open your heart to His presence and the love He pours out, especially when you feel most alone.

4. **Connect with community.** Isolation intensifies suffering. Even when it's difficult, reach out to trusted believers who can sit with you in your pain, as Job's friends did initially (before they started talking).

5. **Look for growth, not escape.** Ask God to show you how He might be using this season to develop perseverance, character, and hope in your life.

Reflection Questions:

1. When have you experienced God's love being "poured out" in the midst of suffering? How did it change your perspective?

2. How might your current struggles be developing perseverance, character, and hope in your life?

3. In what ways has suffering given you a deeper understanding of Christ, who suffered for us?

4. How can you embrace God's presence rather than just seeking answers during difficult seasons?

Scripture References for Further Study:

- Psalm 34:18
- 2 Corinthians 1:3-7
- Romans 8:18
- 1 Peter 4:12-13
- Hebrews 12:1-3
- Isaiah 43:1-2
- Psalm 23:4
- Revelation 21:4

8

HOPE IN FRONT OF ME

EMBRACING GOD'S PROMISE FOR YOUR FUTURE

*"There's a place at the end of the storm you finally find,
where the hurt and the tears and the pain all fall behind"*
—Danny Gokey, *Hope In Front of Me*

Jeremiah 29:11 (CSB)

"For I know the plans I have for you—this is the Lord's declaration—plans for your well-being, not for disaster, to give you a future and a hope."

Christmas is the only Christian holy day that is also a major secular holiday worldwide. The result is two different celebrations observed by millions in different ways, yet with the same symbols, festivities, and songs. People everywhere listen to both *"Joy to the World"* and *"Have a Holly Jolly Christmas,"* promoting Christmas as time off for family, giving, and peace to the world.

CHAPTER 8

How does someone who preaches hope every Sunday reach such a point of hopelessness?

Yet non-religious people cannot help the intrusion of traditional Christmas themes into their lives, even if uninvited. When they hear "Hark the Herald Angels Sing," they encounter profound theology:

- Christ the everlasting Lord!
- Offspring of a Virgin's womb
- Hail the heaven-born Prince of Peace!
- Hail the Son of Righteousness!
- Born to give them second birth

Can you imagine a child asking a secular parent what all that means?

As a Christian believer, sharing the virtues of the day with secular society is fine with me. Lights, festivities, family gatherings, and gift-giving are good for everyone. And I recognize that because of the commercial indispensability of Christmas, it will remain a secular festival.

My fear, however, is that its true roots have become increasingly hidden from the mass of the population, including professing Christians.

We believe that light in darkness comes from the Christian understanding that the world's hope comes from outside itself. Yet we're experiencing a time when darkness has shunned the light, leaving the world—and people who should be full of hope—increasingly hopeless. Even without saying it explicitly, many are living as if they have no reason to hope.

Many people are reeling with discouragement—or far worse mental health issues. The statistics are staggering. CDC research shows that 31 percent of Americans reported anxiety and depression during the pandemic, and 11 percent considered suicide. According to the *Journal of the American Medical Association,* that's a three-fold increase in "the rate of depression in US adults." Medical Doctor Brennan Spiegel said, "The pandemic has also spawned a mental health crisis beyond anything I have seen in 25 years of caring for patients."[11]

Without dwelling on the suicide uptick over the last four to five years, let me address this year's statistics regarding depression and mental illness.

Boston University led a study involving data from 1,441 respondents to a COVID-19 Life Stressors Impact on Mental Health and Well-Being survey. The survey was based on the Patient Health Questionnaire-9, the most commonly used self-administered depression screening tool. The results showed that:

- 27.8% of adults reported depression symptoms, compared with 8.5% before the pandemic
- Depression rates increased from 10.1% of women and 6.9% of men before the pandemic to 22.2% of women and 21.9% of men during the pandemic
- Respondents who were married had an 18.3% rate of depression symptoms, compared with:
    - 31.5% in those who were widowed, divorced, or separated,
    - 39.8% in those who never married, and
    - 37.7% in those living with a partner.

The survey results reveal that depression rates more than doubled after previous large-scale traumatic events such as the September 11, 2001, terrorist attacks and Ebola outbreaks. The researchers also predicted that the prevalence of mental illness will spread along with the virus over time and that the symptoms will be long-lasting. *"Post-COVID-19 plans should account for the probable increase in mental illness to come, particularly among at-risk populations,"* the authors wrote. The lead author, doctoral student Catherine Ettman, said, *"We would hope that these findings promote creating a society where a robust safety net exists."*[12]

There is a point there: Loneliness and weak social connections have the same effect on your health as smoking 15 cigarettes a day! So I don't want to dismiss the statement about creating a society with a robust safety net. However, here's the problem: the safety net can sometimes leave you in the hands of broken, fragile people no stronger or better off than you are. Community is great—we believe in it, invite you into it, and know the power of not doing life alone. But even within community, our ultimate trust must be beyond mere flesh.

Jeremiah 17:5-8 (NLT)

"This is what the Lord says: 'Cursed are those who put their trust in mere humans, who rely on human strength and turn their hearts away from the Lord. They are like stunted shrubs in the desert, with no hope for the future. They will live in the barren wilderness, in an uninhabited salty land. But blessed are those who trust in the Lord and have made the Lord their hope and confidence. They are like trees planted along a riverbank, with roots that reach deep into the water. Such trees are not bothered by the heat or worried by long months of drought. Their leaves stay green, and they never stop producing fruit.'"

The meaning couldn't be clearer. Relying on human strength or your own flesh will lead to no hope for the future. The description is one we can understand—barren, salty ground that cannot produce. But what if you trusted in God and put your hope in Him? Your life would become like a tree being watered and nourished that, even during drought seasons, still produces fruit! Do you see that? Trust in the Lord! Hope and confidence in Him!

Jeremiah expressed this another way in Lamentations:

Lamentations 3:17-25 (NLT)

"I have been deprived of peace; I have forgotten what prosperity is. Then I thought, 'My future is lost, as well as my hope from the Lord.' I remember my affliction and my wandering, the bitterness and the gall. I continually remember them and have become depressed. Yet I still dare to hope when I remember this: The faithful love of the Lord never ends! His mercies never cease. Great is his faithfulness; his mercies

begin afresh each morning. I say to myself, 'The Lord is my inheritance; therefore, I will hope in him!' The Lord is good to those who depend on him, to those who search for him."

NASA astronaut Scott Kelly spent a year in space and spoke about the encouragement this passage gave him. Of course, he had an advantage we don't—he spent one year on the International Space Station, which travels at 17,100 miles per hour, orbiting Earth every 90 minutes. That means he saw a sunrise every 90 minutes. From the Cupola Observation Module, Scott witnessed 16 sunrises and 16 sunsets every day.

We too are in an observation module of life every minute. Keep your eyes on the horizon, looking into the face of God, and watch Him renew mercy for you! He is good to those who depend on Him! The Lord's faithfulness is as sure as the sunrise! That begs the question: who is this Lord, and how does hope come from Him?

1 Timothy 4:10 (NIV)

"For this reason we have put our hope in the living God, who is the Savior of all people, especially of those who believe."

That's right! There is a God who lives, who loves, who came to earth in the form of a baby—God incarnate, in human flesh—to save us and give us hope.

Matthew 1:18-25 (NLT)

"This is how Jesus the Messiah was born. His mother, Mary, was engaged to be married to Joseph. But before the marriage took place, while she was still a virgin, she became pregnant through the power of the Holy Spirit. Joseph, to whom she was engaged, was a righteous man and did not want to disgrace her publicly, so he decided to break the engagement quietly. As he considered this, an angel of the Lord appeared to him in a dream. 'Joseph, son of David,' the angel said, 'do not be afraid to take Mary as your wife. For the child within her was conceived by the Holy Spirit. And she will have a son, and you are to name him Jesus, for he will save his people from their sins.'

CHAPTER 8

"All of this occurred to fulfill the Lord's message through his prophet: 'Look! The virgin will conceive a child! She will give birth to a son, and they will call him Immanuel, which means "God is with us."'"

"When Joseph woke up, he did as the angel of the Lord commanded and took Mary as his wife. But he did not have sexual relations with her until her son was born. And Joseph named him Jesus."

You should notice two things:

First, His name has meaning. Many of us ponder the meaning of names and why people name their children as they do. Craig Groeschel shared a list of unfortunate name combinations of actual people:[13]

- One person named their daughter *Eileen Wright*
- Another was named *Lois Price*
- One lady, *Helen,* married a man with the last name Back (after ten years of marriage, he confirmed it was true)
- Perhaps the worst was *Keesha May* who had the last name *Ash*

Nothing unfortunate about Jesus' name at all—it speaks of what He does: save us from our sins!

Second, you might wonder: why wasn't He named *Immanuel?* In the prophecy of the virgin birth in Isaiah 7:14, the prophet declared, *"The Lord himself will give you a sign: The virgin will conceive and give birth to a son, and will call him Immanuel."*

The truth is, there are many names given to Jesus in the Old and New Testaments, and Immanuel is one of them. Isaiah elsewhere prophesied of the Messiah, *"He will be called Wonderful Counselor, Mighty God, Everlasting Father, Prince of Peace"* (Isaiah 9:6), but none of these was His given name.

The prophet Jeremiah writes of *"a King who will reign wisely"* (Jeremiah 23:5), and gives us another name for the coming Messiah: *"And this is the name by which he will be called: 'The LORD is our righteousness'"* (Jeremiah

23:6, ESV). Jesus was never called *"The Lord Our Righteousness"* as a formal name, but we can call Him that!

George Herman Ruth was named George, of course. But we can call him other things while talking about the same person: *"Babe," "the Bambino," "the Sultan of Swat," or "the Colossus of Clout."* Babe Ruth accumulated these names due to his personal history and talent on the baseball field. Similarly, we can call Jesus by His given name, but we can also call Him *"Immanuel."*

Joseph named Him Jesus so we know why He came—to save people from their sins. But I also call Him *Immanuel* because when depression tries to set in, when discouragement closes in, when I'm tempted to feel hopeless, I hear the angel say He shall be called *Immanuel*—because God is with me! That is why I have hope! Hope has arrived! Hope has a name! His name is Jesus! This hope is for now and for the future!

What shatters your hope can differ between individuals. For the Hebrews, it was being exiled to a foreign land and forced to adopt a foreign culture. For some, it's the failure of a business. For others, it may be being turned down for a mortgage loan, plunging them into an abyss. Still others face the death of a visionary breadwinner. Not all hopelessness is one-size-fits-all.

For me, personally, it was a "never thought possible" divorce. Without delving into the details of what happened, what wasn't known by many was the mental and emotional state that became my disposition. I'd accepted a tolerance for loneliness. There was no hope within me that companionship and the God-designed pleasure of life with someone I could fully love—and who would fully love me—would ever happen again.

It wasn't because I didn't want it; there were just too many obstacles. Theological positions for some, doctrinal concerns for others, the incalculable response of the church, and possibly the unspoken thoughts of my children all seemed insurmountable. So I settled, with no hope of change.

After years of being single and telling people I would not remarry, the Lord reestablished His place in that area of my life. While sitting with a couple

CHAPTER 8

from our church at a local coffee shop, the question of remarriage came up. Immediately I said, "That is not happening."

As quick as I finished the sentence, a sound like a wooden board being snapped in my head got my attention. The sound was alarming, but what was more pronounced was the surge of sensation in my soul. I was fully aware something remarkable had happened, and I needed to pay attention to what was happening. That wasn't "my head"; God was getting my attention.

As surely as I write this, what seemed to be audible words came to me: "That is an area of lordship you have taken in your life." I'd heard the Lord's voice before, so I knew it was Him.

To my shame, the rest of the conversation with the couple became indistinct—God was speaking, and He had my attention.

Without being rude, I brought the meeting to a close. I needed to get to my vehicle so I could pray and ask the Lord if that was truly Him. That's exactly what I did as soon as my Ford Fusion's door closed.

"Lord, if that was you, make it undeniable."

My drive from the coffee shop to my office is about six miles. With no conscious thought of what would happen next, I headed that way—until I couldn't continue. Approximately two miles into the drive, I was flooded with such an emotional outburst of tears that I had to pull over. The Lord was affirming what He had said.

Honestly, hearing from the Lord and knowing it was Him didn't cause me anxiety. The next steps did! I had said for so long to my pastor, my elders, my children, and my congregation that I wasn't going to remarry. And now the Lord was saying otherwise. How would I approach this?

After days of prayer and contemplation, I formed a plan.

My first conversation needed to be with a friend, Mark Sligar, and my pastor, Dave Patterson. Mark has been a trusted friend for many years and serves as Executive Pastor of The Father's House in Vacaville, California. Dave is the lead pastor and a wise, trusted mentor.

So I flew up to meet them without revealing my main reason. It wasn't uncommon for me to fly to Vacaville for meetings and mentoring opportunities. After a few days, I shared with Mark and Dave what I'd heard from the Lord. I was really hoping they would say, "Are you sure? That doesn't seem right for you."

But to my surprise, they both received it as great news and didn't doubt the message.

Check!

Next step?

For almost seven years, my children had heard me say I wasn't getting married again. I had no idea how any of the five would respond. I spoke to each of them personally. My sons were more accepting than my daughters. Though their acceptance wasn't quite celebratory, they were supportive. Check!

Next step?

The elders of Church For The City (CTC) were very accepting, prayerful, and excited about the possibility of my happiness. They believed the church would feel the same. Check!

All those worthy of consultation had been consulted. What lay before me was: who was to be my wife?

When I sent a letter to my intercessors informing them of this possibility, Jane Bell, a dear friend, asked about my thoughts regarding a prospective wife. We discussed several options for finding her—some with humor. I recall ending that part of our conversation with these words:

"I know this doesn't happen anymore, but it is in the Bible. I wish I could see someone, and she loves me, and I love her, just like Isaac and Rebecca.

CHAPTER 8

Again, I know that doesn't happen anymore, but it is in the Bible, and I sure hope it can happen for me."

I concluded with laughter. From that conversation, months passed with no prospect I knew was from the Lord.

The second Sunday of June 2017, as I was greeting congregants at the door after services, my Spanish pastor, Juan Escobar, informed me that his sister was visiting. I replied with "okay." Then he asked if I remembered her—his sister Virginia. With a tinge of dishonesty, I said yes.

As I looked into the lobby to see how many more people were coming out for me to greet, my eyes fell on a woman unfamiliar to me. She was stunningly beautiful. My excitement to greet her grew as she approached. When she was just steps away, Pastor Juan said, "Pastor, this is my sister Virginia." I was literally speechless.

After greeting Virginia awkwardly, I made an internal decision to get more information about her when I returned from India, where I was leaving that evening to return in about ten days. From that meeting at the door of CTC, and through communication while I was in India, I became convinced that Virginia was the picture of restored hope the Lord had brought into my life. On our first date, Virginia told me she had informed her family that Sunday that I would marry her.

Here it is in Virginia's own words:

Joy comes when you least expect it. I had been single for twelve years and attended a small Spanish-speaking church with my dad. One of my brothers had been attending Church For The City and was always inviting me to attend a service. On Sunday, June 11, 2017, he texted to remind me that I had said I would go. I stepped into CTC, when Pastor Tyrone got up to speak. I told my brother that his Pastor was easy on the eyes and easy on the ears! I loved his voice and the way he carried himself. I soon forgot about that as I sat and listened to him deliver the message. It was anointed and powerful and I thought it was way too short. After the service my brother kept stalling to walk out and I was ready to go get lunch. Pastor Tyrone was outside talking to people as they were leaving. When we got to the door my brother talked to him and introduced me to him. He turned and looked at me and reached out to hug me but didn't say anything, really. I took his hand and hugged him back. As I did, I knew what the Holy Spirit deposited in me. As I walked away from the building with my brother and his wife—while they were deciding where we would go eat—I looked over at them with a giggle and said, "Your pastor is going to marry me!" On September 23, 2017, he proposed to me, and we were married December 22, 2017

You see, Virginia had received a prophetic promise when she was young that she would marry a pastor. A failed and abusive marriage of over twenty years, followed by ten years of being single, had caused her to give up hope that this word was truly from the Lord. Yet a chance meeting on a Sunday, after the Lord had told me what was to be done, brought two people together—proving God is a restorer to the hopeless.

The same God who proved to me that He sees us in dark places was the same God who sparked hope in Virginia's life that the Lord would fulfill His word.

Virginia has proven to be the greatest gift of my life outside of my salvation. Every anxiety, every speck of hopelessness, and every prayer regarding a wife has been answered in my love for her.

You can absolutely discover God's light in dark places. Hope—now and in the future—is no fairy tale. Hope has a name: Jesus! The One who was, who is, and who is to come does come, and He brings hope with Him!

Psalm 33:20-22 (CSB)

"We wait for the Lord; he is our help and shield. For our hearts rejoice in him because we trust in his holy name. May your faithful love rest on us, Lord, for we put our hope in you."

Like me, Israel needed hope. Their present situation was bleak. They were not in their homeland. Rather, they were displaced by God's providence for

CHAPTER 8

discipline. There in the land of their enemy—Babylon—everything about their culture, practices, and worship was violated. And because of their rebellion against God and lack of hearing His Word, they were dull to the promise of God meant for them.

Among the prophets taken from their homeland was Jeremiah. It was this Jeremiah who Daniel discovered had stated that the people of God from Israel would be in this foreign country for 70 years.

Just imagine it for a moment—you being taken from your home and all its familiarity and comforts and placed in a place you have never been, know no one, cannot speak the language, and don't know the culture or what is proper. I do much foreign travel, and I can tell you: when I get frustrated, my comforting thought is that it's only nine days or less—not 70 years!

Jeremiah 29:10-11 (CSB)

> *"For this is what the Lord says: 'When seventy years for Babylon are complete, I will attend to you and will confirm my promise concerning you to restore you to this place. For I know the plans I have for you'—this is the Lord's declaration—'plans for your well-being, not for disaster, to give you a future and a hope.'"*

What is important to know is that when Jeremiah declared the good of God for them, he informed them that they needed to build homes, take wives, and plant gardens. The instructions were given while they were suffering in a foreign land! None of them could foresee a future in that place, or even in their own homeland. Responding to this prophetic declaration from Jeremiah was a far stretch for the most holy—no less the common man of Israel.

Here's what we need to understand—Jeremiah had a message of hope for them before the situation got worse—and it did! When he spoke these words, only a few hundred people had been exiled, and they were not quite three years into their captivity.

When I was in Johannesburg for the first time in late 2006, my host, Bill Scheidler, a spiritual father to me, took me to the theater to see a newly released film titled *Faith Like Potatoes*.

The true story of Angus Buchan, who was a white Zambian farmer of Scottish origin, emigrates to escape political unrest and worrying land reforms. He looks south for a better life. The film follows Buchan and his family's move to South Africa and chronicles his Christian faith.

With nothing more than a trailer in the untamed bush, the Buchan family struggles to settle in their new homeland. Faced with ever-mounting challenges, hardships and personal turmoil, Buchan quickly spirals down into a life consumed by anger. Finally, his wife convinces him to attend a local church, where the testimony of other farmers influences his decision to give his life to Jesus Christ.

His outlook on God and life takes a complete turnaround, and supernatural occurrences begin to happen when Angus prays in faith.

The heart of the movie, however, is this: while a drought was devastating the land, the word of the Lord to Angus was to plant potatoes. Traditionally, Angus was a maize and cattle farmer. Scientists, other farmers, and people from the Zulu tribe who knew the land warned him not to do so. The drought would not allow the potatoes to germinate, no less produce a crop. Because of the unprecedented drought, planting potatoes would be a massive risk. Believing he was led by the Lord, he planted potatoes in the dry dust. When harvest time came, there was a crop of giant potatoes. He acknowledged the word of the Lord before he witnessed the evidence: *"I have plans for your well-being, not for disaster, to give you a future and a hope.'"*

I recall when COVID news hit the country, many of us—including me—were saying, "Let's wait a week, see where this goes, and if it turns out to be a shutdown, we'll prepare to reopen by Easter." Well, you know how that went!

Often we use verse 11—*"For I know the plans I have for you...plans for your well-being, not for disaster, to give you a future and a hope"*—to encourage people when they're in the midst of trouble. While it's always good to encourage people when we can, God is not reactive but proactive!

In other words, God doesn't see you in a bad situation and then determine how to make it better. The God we know and serve doesn't need to see it happen. He knows what you will face, allows you to face it for whatever reason and purposes He knows to be good—and yet has already acted for what will prove to be a good future!

FOREKNOWLEDGE is an aspect of God's omniscience. All things past, present, future—external and internal—material, intellectual, and spiritual—are open to Him and known by Him.

Isaiah 46:9-10 (CSB)

"For I am God, and there is no other; I am God, and no one is like me. I declare the end from the beginning, and from long ago what is not yet done, saying: my plan will take place, and I will do all my will."

I don't know the unknown, but the all-knowing God does!

So here we have it: The Lord tells Jeremiah it will get worse before it gets better—but they should have hope. "I know the plans I have for them! My plans cannot be changed or ruined! It is good, for their future, and will give them hope!"

Why was this so important? Because like many of us, they wanted to avoid bad news. I get it—I don't want to hear of unavoidable troubling situations. To cause further hopelessness, there were prophets among them saying that what Jeremiah was saying was not true.

Jeremiah 29:8-9 (NLT)

"This is what the Lord of Heaven's Armies, the God of Israel, says: 'Do not let your prophets and fortune-tellers who are with you in the land of Babylon trick you. Do not listen to their dreams, because they are telling you lies in my name. I have not sent them,' says the Lord."

We need to be conscious of the same today. It is not that all negative circumstances are from God, but some things do have divine purpose. Challenges, trials, and tests can serve a great purpose in what the Lord is doing in our future, as was the case with the people of God from Israel. What I also know is that when you honor God and trust Him, there is no reason to fear bad news.

Psalm 112:6-7 (ESV)

> *"For the righteous will never be moved; he will be remembered forever. He is not afraid of bad news; his heart is firm, trusting in the Lord."*
>
> *"Their circumstances will never shake them, and they will not live in fear or dread of what may come, for their hearts are firm, ever secure in their faith."*

Why? I know the plans He has for me! They are for good, not evil, and for a future hope!

> *"God doesn't see you in a bad situation and then determine how to make it better. God is not reactive but proactive!"*

Two Truths About God's Plans for You

1. **His plans are for YOU!** Personalize it! Each of us has a unique set of problems and situations. My life is not your life, and vice versa. Remember, God is personal! He knows you, thinks of you, loves you, and plans for you!

Psalm 139:1-4

> *"Lord, you know everything there is to know about me. You perceive every movement of my heart and soul, and you understand my every thought before it even enters my mind. You are so intimately aware of me, Lord. You read my heart like an open book and you know all the words I'm*

about to speak before I even start a sentence! You know every step I will take before my journey even begins."

2. **His plans are for YOUR good!** Often we see what we're experiencing and don't see the promise. See it, and hold onto it through the process. It is never a bad plan from a good and loving God.

Psalm 34:8 (NKJV)

"Oh, taste and see that the Lord is good; Blessed is the man who trusts in Him!"

Psalm 31:19 (CSB)

"How great is your goodness, which you have stored up for those who fear you. In the presence of everyone you have acted for those who take refuge in you."

Don't judge the rest of your life from this current season!

The challenge: If you can't change it and God has allowed it, then find out how to prosper in it!

That's exactly what the Lord told the Israelites to do in Babylon. They couldn't change their situation—*God had allowed it for a purpose.* Their future was good and planned by God. So in the meantime, make the most of this life.

Jeremiah 29:4-7 (NLT)

"This is what the Lord of Heaven's Armies, the God of Israel, says to all the captives he has exiled to Babylon from Jerusalem: 'Build homes, and plan to stay. Plant gardens, and eat the food they produce. Marry and have children. Then find spouses for them so that you may have many grandchildren. Multiply! Do not dwindle away! And work for the peace and prosperity of the city where I sent you into exile. Pray to the Lord for it, for its welfare will determine your welfare.'"

Stop sulking!

Live life! Love people! Love your city!

Be peaceful, and work for peace!

Get your harps off the willows *(Psalm 137)*—Rejoice, praise, and worship the God of your salvation!

Will you put your trust in Him? My prayer for you is from these final verses:

Romans 15:13 (NLT)

"I pray that God, the source of hope, will fill you completely with joy and peace because you trust in him. Then you will overflow with confident hope through the power of the Holy Spirit."

2 Thessalonians 2:16-17 (NLT)

"Now may our Lord Jesus Christ himself and God our Father, who loved us and by his grace gave us eternal comfort and a wonderful hope, comfort you and strengthen you in every good thing you do and say."

Practical Application

Reflection Questions:

1. In what area of your life do you most need to remember that God has "hope in front of you"?

2. How has God turned what seemed like a hopeless situation into a testimony of His faithfulness in your life?

3. What promises from God's Word can you hold onto during times when hope seems distant?

4. How might God be calling you to "build homes" and "plant gardens" in a difficult season instead of just waiting for it to end?

Scripture References for Further Study:

- Isaiah 40:31
- Hebrews 6:19-20
- Romans 5:3-5
- Psalm 33:18-22
- 1 Peter 1:3-5
- Lamentations 3:21-24
- Proverbs 23:18
- Titus 2:13

ACKNOWLEDGEMENTS

Thank you to Carl Dobrowolski, Bill Giarratana, Emily Loomis, and the entire team at Goodwill Media Services Corporation, **www.goodwillmedia-services.com,** for giving vision, shape, and direction to this book. What began as thoughts in my head has become a coherent offering that I trust will speak to people for generations to come.

Thank you to the staff of Church For The City. Each one of you has been incredibly encouraging and supportive throughout the writing of this book. I am deeply grateful for your love for me and your unwavering passion for CTC and the kingdom of God.

Particularly, I want to thank Tyrone D. Jones, who has shown honor to me as his father and pastor, and who has championed everything I've attempted to do for the kingdom.

Joel Jimenez, my Project Manager, has worked diligently and served faithfully in executing every aspect of all things *In His Grip Media*.

ACKNOWLEDGEMENTS

Tiara Kandy Ray, who served as my Executive Administrator for many years, including the conception of this book—there is nothing I ask of Kandy that she won't do, and always with joy.

And finally, Marquia Horney, my current Executive Administrator. Marquia has guarded my time, been intentional with my schedule, and made me more efficient as pastor, leader, and author.

A massive thanks is owed to Rick Zorehkey, of Convoy of Hope, and Blaine and Ramsey Morris, friends and members of CTC, who offered me their vacation homes—quiet spaces where I could think, pray, and to receive inspiration to write.

I'm also grateful for the generous friends who read the manuscript, offered brilliant suggestions, and those who endorsed this book at their own peril.

With much gratitude, I acknowledge Pastor Mark Driscoll for giving sound counsel, for setting me up legally, and for financially investing in my dream. Jeff Howie, for being a great friend and theological balance. Bob MacGregor, a longtime mentor, champion, and friend. Rhett Stallworth, for his thoughtful contribution and editing support. And to my prayer intercessors at Church For The City—thank you for praying for me regularly, diligently, and passionately.

The children and grandchildren the Lord has blessed Virginia and me with—and given us an opportunity to parent together—will carry for generations what we have hoped to instill. Jermaine and Cathy, Alex and Liana, Tyrone and Karina, Eli and Laura, Tecia, Tiffany and Jimmy, Junior and Natalie, Malachi, and Norman and Supriya—thank you! I love you all more than you know. If all I have to show for this life here on earth is who each of you are and will become, my joy will be full.

Finally, Church For The City—what a great church! Thank you for allowing me to teach and practice what you've read in this book, but even more, thank you for the opportunity to walk with you as we learn together from the pages of Scripture. The real-life stories here are part of who we are as a

ACKNOWLEDGEMENTS

church—and who you have allowed me to be, as I shepherd you from here to eternity.

For from Him and through Him and to Him are all things. To Him be glory forever. Amen. *(Romans 11:36)*

In His Grip,
Tyrone P Jones

ENDNOTES

[1] Juergen Moltmann, *Theology of Hope: On the Ground and the Implications of a Christian Eschatology*, trans. James W. Leitch (London: SCM Press, 1967).

[2] L. Frank Baum, *The Wonderful Wizard of Oz* (Chicago: George M. Hill Company, 1900).

[3] Erma Bombeck, *If Life Is a Bowl of Cherries, What Am I Doing in the Pits?* (New York: McGraw-Hill, 1978).

[4] Tyler VanderWeele, "On the Promotion of Human Flourishing," *Proceedings of the National Academy of Sciences* 114, no. 31 (2017): 8148–8156.

[5] Charles Wesley, "Eternal Light! Eternal Light!," in *The United Methodist Hymnal*, no. 301 (Nashville: The United Methodist Publishing House, 1989).

[6] Walter Chalmers Smith, "Immortal, Invisible, God Only Wise," in *The Hymnal 1982*, no. 423 (New York: Church Publishing, 1985).

[7] Quoted in E.M. Blaiklock, *The Positive Power of Jesus Christ* (London: Hodder & Stoughton, 1984), 45.

[8] Malcolm Muggeridge, attributed quote. Original source uncertain; possibly referenced in *Imprimis* or *Catholic Insight*. Specific citation unverified.

[9] C.S. Lewis, *The Screwtape Letters* (New York: HarperOne, 2001), 3.

[10] Henry Venn, letter to the Countess of Huntingdon, 1797, cited in Martyn Lloyd-Jones, *Spiritual Depression: Its Causes and Cure* (Grand Rapids: Eerdmans, 1965).

ENDNOTES

[11] Brennan Spiegel, "COVID-19's Impact on Mental Health," *UCLA Health Newsroom*, September 2020.

[12] Catherine K. Ettman et al., "Prevalence of Depression Symptoms in US Adults Before and After the COVID-19 Pandemic," *JAMA Network Open* 3, no. 9 (2020): e2019686.

[13] Craig Groeschel, referenced from *Summit Life* broadcast on the Truth Network, 2023. Exact episode and timestamp recommended for formal citation.